THE
WISDOM OF
JAMES
ALLEN

All titles in this series

The Wisdom of James Allen
The Wisdom of Joseph Murphy
The Wisdom of Napoleon Hill
The Wisdom of Robert Collier
The Wisdom of Wallace D. Wattles

THE
WISDOM OF
JAMES
ALLEN

edited and introduced
by Mitch Horowitz

Published 2020 by Gildan Media LLC
aka G&D Media
www.GandDmedia.com

THE WISDOM OF JAMES ALLEN. Introduction, Chapter Notes, and Timeline,
copyright © 2020 by Mitch Horowitz

Front Cover design by David Rheinhardt of Pyrographx

Interior design by Meghan Day Healey of Story Horse, LLC

Library of Congress Cataloging-in-Publication Data is available upon request

ISBN: 978-1-7225-0148-8

10   9   8   7   6   5   4   3   2   1

Contents

Working-Class Sage
The Power and Progress of James Allen

INTRODUCTION BY MITCH HOROWITZ

In a writing career that lasted just over a decade, English essayist, moralist, and mystic James Allen (1864–1921) revolutionized the field of modern inspirational literature. Before his death from tuberculosis at age 47, Allen produced the enormously popular meditation *As a Man Thinketh* and combined themes of social reform, Victorian self-reliance, and New Thought metaphysics like no author before or since.

Allen's few years of output, ranging from the publication of his first book in 1901 to his death in early 1912, resulted in nearly twenty books, the launch of two magazines, and a countless range of letters, poems, and articles. The British seeker drank deeply from Eastern spirituality (he was among the first Westerners to popularize principles of Buddhism), American motivational and mind-power philosophy, and the rock-ribbed moralism of Victorian England, where he grew up in the shadow of factories and poverty.

His era was one in which Victorian readers were inspired by works like "Invictus" by William Ernest Henley (1849–1903), who was twenty years Allen's elder:

> Out of the night that covers me
> Black as the pit from pole to pole,
> I thank whatever gods may be
> For my unconquerable soul.
>
> In the fell clutch of circumstance,
> I have not winced nor cried aloud.
> Under the bludgeonings of chance
> My head is bloody, but unbowed.
>
> Beyond this place of wrath and tears
> Looms but the Horror of the shade,
> And yet the menace of the years
> Finds, and shall find me, unafraid.
>
> It matters not how strait the gate,
> How charged with punishments the scroll,
> I am the master of my fate:
> I am the captain of my soul.

As you read the works in this collection—which I have structured to capture not only Allen's mystical but also his moral concerns—you will detect his ability to combine the ideal of the British "stiff upper lip" with the insights of New Thought, Buddhism, Confucianism, and mystical Christianity. He may be the only writer for whom this is true. Allen was also a social reformer: he was a vegetarian (an influence from Buddhism), an early advocate for humane treatment of animals, and a supporter of laws protecting workers and promoting social equity.

All this arose from the brief career of a man who lost his father at age fifteen and had to quit school for factory work to ensure his family's survival. As important as anything that he wrote, Allen provided a living example of his philosophy of moral and material progress. That is why I have titled this introduction "Working-Class Sage." That is what Allen is to me—and his life story should be better known to the millions of readers who swear by his signature book *As a Man Thinketh*.

James Allen was born to a working-class home on November 28, 1864 in the industrial town of Leicester, in central England. His mother, Martha, could neither read nor write. His father, William, was a factory knitter who maintained a small manufacturing business. The eldest of three brothers, James was a bookish and gentle boy, doted upon by his father, who cultivated his taste in books and philosophy.

A downturn in the textile trade drove William out of business, and in 1879 he traveled to New York City to look for new work. His plan was to get settled and pay for the rest of the family to join him. But the unthinkable occurred. On the brink of the Christmas season, just after James had turned fifteen, word came back to the home that its patriarch was dead. William had been found robbed and murdered two days after reaching New York. His battered body, with its pockets emptied, lay in a city hospital.

James's mother, Martha, a woman who could not read or write, found herself in charge of James and his two younger brothers. The family had no means of support. "Young Jim" would have to leave school and work as a factory knitter if the Allens were to survive and remain intact.

The teenager had been his father's favorite. An avid reader, James had spent hours questioning his father about life, death, religion, politics, and Shakespeare. "My boy," William told him, "I'll make a scholar of you." Those hopes seemed gone.

James took up employment locally as a framework knitter, a job that occupied his energies for the next nine years. He sometimes worked fifteen-hour days. But even amid the strains of factory life, he retained the dignified, studious bearing that his father had cultivated. When his workmates went out drinking, or caught up on sleep, Allen studied and read two to three hours a day. Coworkers called him "the Saint" and "the Parson."

Allen read through his father's collected works of Shakespeare, as well as books of ethics and religion. He grew determined to discover the "central purpose" of life. At age twenty-four he found the book that finally seemed to reveal it to him: *The Light of Asia* by Edwin Arnold. The epic poem introduced Allen, along with a generation of Victorians, to the ideas of Buddhism. Under its influence, Allen came to believe that the true aim of all religion was self-development and inner refinement.

Shortly after discovering *The Light of Asia*, Allen experienced a turning point in his outer life, as well. Around 1889 he found new employment in London as a private secretary and stationer—friendlier vocations to the bookish man than factory work. In London he met his wife and intellectual partner, Lily Louisa Oram. They wed in 1895. The following year, Lily gave birth to the couple's daughter and only child, Nora.

By this time, Allen had developed an impassioned interest in the world's spiritual philosophies, poring over the works of John Milton, Ralph Waldo Emerson, Walt Whitman, and early translations of the *Bhagavad Gita*, *Tao Te Ching*, and the sayings of Confucius and Buddha. He marveled over the commonalities in the world's religions. "The man who says, 'My religion is true, and my neighbor's is false,' has not yet discovered the truth in his own religion," he wrote, "for when a man has done that, he will see the Truth in all religions."

He soon grew interested in the ideas of America's burgeoning New Thought culture through the work of Ralph Waldo Trine, Christian D. Larson, and Orison Swett Marden. His reading of New Thought literature sharpened his spiritual outlook—in particular his idea that our thoughts are causative and determine our destiny.

By 1898, Allen found an outlet for his spiritual and social interests when he began writing for the magazine, *The Herald of the Golden Age*. The journal was a pioneering voice for vegetarianism and humane treatment of animals, and also highlighted metaphysics and practical spirituality. Allen's writing for *The Herald of the Golden Age* commenced a period of feverish creative activity.

By 1901, he published his first book of spiritual philosophy, *From Poverty to Power*. The work extolled the creative agencies of the mind, placing an equal emphasis on Christian-based ethics and New Thought motivation. In 1902, Allen launched his own spiritual magazine, *The Light of Reason*—a tribute to Arnold's title—later redubbed *The Epoch*.

The following year, Allen produced the book that made his name known worldwide: the short, immensely powerful meditation, *As a Man Thinketh*, which is reprinted in full in this collection. The title came from Proverbs 23:7: "As he thinketh in his heart, so is he." In Allen's eyes, that brief statement laid out his core philosophy—that a person's thought, if not the cause of his circumstances, is the cause of *himself*, and shapes the tenor of his life.

As the book's popularity rose, the phrase "as a man thinketh" became the informal motto of the New Thought movement, adopted and repeated by motivational writers throughout the century. Indeed, twentieth-century New-Thoughters frequently borrowed, cross-referenced, and repurposed one another's language—sometimes to the point where an original reference, or its meaning, got lost. This was the case with Allen's title phrase. Read in context in Proverbs 23:6–7, the precept "as a man thinketh" is not a principle of cause-and-effect thinking, but rather a caution against covetousness and hypocrisy:

Eat thou not the bread of him that hath an evil eye, neither desire thou his dainty meats:

For as he thinketh in his heart, so is he: Eat and drink, saith he to thee; but his heart is not with thee.

This kind of misunderstanding was common in New Thought. The early positive thinkers were passionate to describe their ideas as the fulfillment of ancient doctrines. Hence, they tended to retrofit the positivity gospel to Scripture and other antique sources, sometimes ignoring the context of favored passages.

Regardless, Allen's book was otherwise marked by memorable, aphoristic passages, which have withstood the passage of time. *As a Man Thinketh* defined achievement in deeply personal terms: "You will become as small as your controlling desire; as great as your dominant aspiration." Toward the end of *As a Man Thinketh*, Allen wrote in a manner that amounted to autobiography:

Here is a youth hard pressed by poverty and labor; confined long hours in an unhealthy workshop; unschooled, and lacking all the arts of refinement. But he dreams of better things: he thinks of intelligence, of refinement, of grace and beauty. He conceives of, mentally builds up, an ideal condition of life; vision of a wider liberty and a larger scope takes possession of him; unrest urges him to action, and he utilizes all his spare time and means, small though they are, to the development of his latent powers

and resources. Very soon so altered has his mind become
that the workshop can no longer hold him.

Although I grew up in circumstances hardly compara-
ble to the brutalities of England's "dark Satanic mills," I,
like many readers, knew struggle and felt that Allen's pen
expressed the progress of my own life.

The same year that he wrote *As a Man Thinketh*, 1903, Allen
produced another book—less well known but equally powerful in scope and practicality: *All These Things Added*,
excerpts of which appear in this collection.

All These Things Added is consummate James Allen, and
deserves special mention. The concise work encapsulates an
entire philosophy of life. In *All These Things Added*, Allen
created a method of day-to-day living designed to bring personal fulfillment and self-realization. He based it on his inter-
pretation of *Matthew* 6:33:

> *But seek ye first the kingdom of God, and his*
> *righteousness;*
>
> *and all these things shall be added unto you.*

The book captures Allen's struggle—and all of ours—to
live by the principle of reaching beyond our grasp. And of
seeking to produce more than we grab. Perhaps more than
any other book, *All These Things Added* reflects the personal
search that marked Allen's life.

*   *   *

With the publication and success of these two books, the Allen family moved to the southern English costal town of Ilfracombe, where Allen spent the rest of life. He produced books at a remarkable pace—often more than one a year.

With Lily as his partner, Allen hosted discussion groups on metaphysical themes, continued publishing *The Epoch*, and spent long periods of time in nature, taking early morning walks and exploring the coastal highlands. His life assumed a meticulous routine of meditating, writing, walking the coast, and gardening. Friends sensed that he was living out the simple, ascetic ideal of one of his literary heroes, Leo Tolstoy.

For all the vigor of his output, Allen was in fragile health. Lily wrote of her husband's health faltering in late 1911. On January 24, 1912, Allen died at home in Ilfracombe at age 47, probably of tuberculosis. His body was cremated—a funerary choice that was then unpopular in the West but reflected the seeker's fealty to Eastern traditions.

Lily continued to publish her husband's remaining manuscripts, to work on her own books, and to edit and publish *The Epoch*. She also founded her own New Thought-oriented society, the Union of Right Thinking. She died on February 14, 1952. The Allens' daughter, Nora, a Spiritualist and later a devout Roman Catholic, died July 18, 1976.

The true legacy of James Allen is that the British author established a philosophy of self-advancement set within a framework of Eastern mysticism, Christian asceticism, and

American motivation. He combined these elements like no other writer. His values were simple, clear traits of thrift, reliability, hard work, respect of one's neighbor and employer, along with a deeply held belief in the unseen power of the individual who, through the proper exercise of thought, could radically transform his circumstances.

Allen was simultaneously the Victorian moralist and the searching mystic. The path to personal greatness, he believed, is found in eschewing self-indulgence, pursuing a modest existence of basic needs, and tirelessly exercising the control of your thoughts to minimize what is cruel and petty, while cultivating ideals of tolerance, generosity, kindness, and, above all, belief in self. Through these methods, Allen insisted, you can realize untapped powers and resources. This is the path he walked from factory orphan to internationally known writer.

Although Allen loved the greenery of the British landscape, his work found its greatest popularity outside his native land. In an obituary of January 27, 1912, the *Ilfracombe Chronicle* noted: "Mr. Allen's books . . . are perhaps better known abroad, especially in America."

Indeed, the twentieth century's leading American writers of motivational thought—from Napoleon Hill to Norman Vincent Peale—read and noted the influence of *As a Man Thinketh*. Dale Carnegie said the book had "a lasting and profound effect on my life." The cofounder of Alcoholics Anonymous, Bob Smith, called it a favorite. The black-nationalist pioneer Marcus Garvey embraced the book's do-for-self ethic and adapted the slogan "As Man Thinks So Is He" on the cover of his newspaper *Blackman*. In years ahead, the book's influence showed up in myriad places: An adolescent Michael Jackson told a friend that it was his "favorite book in the world"; NFL Hall-of-Famer Curtis Martin credited *As a Man Thinketh* with helping him overcome pain and injury; businessman and Oprah Winfrey partner Stedman Graham said Allen's work helped him attain "real freedom."

The full impact of *As a Man Thinketh* and Allen's work in general can best be seen in the successive generations of readers who embraced his aphoristic lessons in directing one's thoughts to higher aims and to understanding success as the outer manifestation of inner development. "Men do not attract that which they want," Allen told readers, "but that which they are."

In that sense, Allen attracted a vast following who mirrored the ordinary circumstances from which he arose—and whose hopes for a better, nobler existence were redirected back to them in writing that bore the mark of his experience.

In 1913, Lily Allen summarized her husband's mission in a preface to one of his posthumously published manuscripts:

He never wrote *theories*, or for the sake of writing; but he wrote when he had a message, and it became a message *only when he had lived it out in his own life*, and knew that it was good. Thus he wrote *facts*, which he had proven by practice.

I

"The World a Reflex of Mental States"

(from *From Poverty to Power*, 1901)

This chapter summarizes James Allen's guiding philosophy: the world is a mirror of self. *Within this principle, Allen discovered and offered to others the source of ultimate power. Even amid the brutalities of industrial Victorian life—Queen Victoria died the year of this essay—Allen found succor, possibility, and dignity through his hard-won understanding of the laws of thought. Venture inward, Allen taught, and you will discover the wellspring of life. From the refinement of your inner being, including your thoughts and inner speech, you can remold the nature of outer circumstance. This solution is always and everywhere available to you.* —MH

The World
a Reflex of Mental States

What you are, so is your world. Everything in the universe is resolved into your own inward experience. It matters little what is without, for it is all a reflection of your own state of consciousness. It matters everything what you are within, for everything without will be mirrored and colored accordingly.

All that you positively know is contained in your own experience; all that you ever will know must pass through the gateway of experience, and so become part of yourself.

Your own thoughts, desires, and aspirations comprise your world, and, to you, all that there is in the universe of beauty and joy and bliss, or of ugliness and sorrow and pain, is contained within yourself. By your own thoughts you make or mar your life, your world, your universe. As you build within by the power of thought, so will your outward life and circumstances shape themselves accordingly.

Whatsoever you harbor in the inmost chambers of your heart will, sooner or later by the inevitable law of reaction, shape itself in your outward life. The soul that is impure, sordid, and selfish is gravitating with unerring precision toward misfortune and catastrophe; the soul that is pure, unselfish, and noble is gravitating with equal precision toward happiness and prosperity. Every soul attracts its own, and nothing can possibly come to it that does not belong to it. To realize this is to recognize the universality of Divine Law. The incidents of every human life, which both make and mar, are drawn to it by the quality and power of its own inner thought-life. Every soul is a complex combination of gathered experiences and thoughts, and the body is but an improvised vehicle for its manifestation. What, therefore, your thoughts are, that is your real self; and the world around, both animate and inanimate, wears the aspect with which your thoughts clothe it. "All that we are is the result of what we have thought; it is founded on our thoughts; it is made up of our thoughts." Thus said Buddha, and it therefore follows that if a man is happy, it is because he dwells in happy thoughts; if miserable, because he dwells in despondent and debilitating thoughts. Whether one be fearful or fearless, foolish or wise, troubled or serene, within that soul lies the cause of its own state or states, and never without. And now I seem to hear a chorus of voices exclaim, "But do you really mean to say that outward circumstances do not affect our minds?" I do not say that, but I say this, and know it to be an infallible truth, *that circumstances can only affect you in so far as you allow them to do so*. You are swayed by circumstances because you have not a right understanding of the nature, use, and power of thought. You believe (and upon this little word *belief* hang all our sorrows and joys) that outward things have the power to make or mar your life; by so doing you submit to those outward things, confess that you are their slave, and they your unconditional master; by so doing, you invest them with a power which they do not, of themselves, possess, and you succumb, in reality, not to the mere circumstances, but to the gloom or gladness, the fear or hope, the strength or weakness, which your thought-sphere has thrown around them.

I knew two men who, at an early age, lost the hard-earned savings of years. One was very deeply troubled, and gave way to chagrin, worry, and despondency. The other, on reading in his morning paper that the bank in which his money was deposited had hopelessly failed, and that he had lost all, quietly and firmly remarked, "Well, it's gone, and trouble and worry won't bring it back, but hard work will." He went to work with renewed vigor, and rapidly became prosperous, while the former man, continuing to mourn the loss of his money, and to grumble at his "bad luck," remained the sport and tool of adverse circumstances, in reality of his own weak and slavish thoughts. The loss of money was a curse to the one because he clothed the event with dark and dreary thoughts; it was a blessing to the other, because he threw around it thoughts of strength, of hope, and renewed endeavor.

If circumstances had the power to bless or harm, they would bless and harm all men alike, but the fact that the same circumstances will be alike good and bad to different souls proves that the good or bad is not in the circumstance, but only in the mind of him that encounters it. When you begin to realize this you will begin to control your thoughts, to regulate and discipline your mind, and to rebuild the inward temple of your soul, eliminating all useless and superfluous material, and incorporating into your being thoughts alone of joy and serenity, of strength and life, of compassion and love, of beauty and immortality; and as you do this you will become joyful and serene, strong and healthy, compassionate and loving, and beautiful with the beauty of immortality.

And as we clothe events with the drapery of our own thoughts, so likewise do we clothe the objects of the visible world around us, and where one sees harmony and beauty, another sees revolting ugliness. An enthusiastic naturalist was one day roaming the country lanes in pursuit of his hobby, and during his rambles came upon a pool of brackish water near a farmyard. As he proceeded to fill a small bottle with the water for the purpose of examination under the microscope, he dilated, with more enthusiasm than discretion, to an uncultivated son of the plough who stood close by, upon the hidden and innumerable wonders contained in the pool, and concluded by saying, "Yes, my friend, within this pool is contained a hundred, nay, a million universes, had we but the sense or the instrument by which we could apprehend them." And the unsophisticated one ponderously remarked, "I know the water be full o' tadpoles, but they be easy to catch."

Where the naturalist, his mind stored with the knowledge of natural facts, saw beauty, harmony, and hidden glory, the mind unenlightened upon those things saw only an offensive mud-puddle.

The wild flower which the casual wayfarer thoughtlessly tramples upon is, to the spiritual eye of the poet, an angelic messenger from the invisible. To the many, the ocean is but a dreary expanse of water on which ships sail and are sometimes wrecked; to the soul of the musician it is a living thing, and he hears, in all its changing moods, divine harmonies. Where the ordinary mind sees disaster and confusion, the mind of the philospher sees the most perfect sequence of cause and effect, and where the materialist sees nothing but endless death, the mystic sees pulsating and eternal life.

And as we clothe both events and objects with our own thoughts, so likewise do we clothe the souls of others in the garments of our thoughts. The suspicious believe everybody to be suspicious; the liar feels secure in the thought that he is not so foolish as to believe that there is such a phenomenon as a strictly truthful person; the envious see envy in every soul; the miser thinks everybody is eager to get his money; he who has subordinated conscience in the making of his wealth sleeps with a revolver under his pillow, wrapt in the delusion that the world is full of conscienceless people who are eager to rob him, and the abandoned sensualist looks upon the saint as a hypocrite. On the other hand, those who dwell in loving thoughts see that in all which calls forth their love and sympathy; the trusting and honest are not troubled by suspicions; the good-natured and charitable who rejoice at the good fortune of others, scarcely know what envy means; and he who has realized the Divine within himself recognizes it in all beings, even in the beasts.

And men and women are confirmed in their mental outlook because of the fact that, by the law of cause and effect, they attract to themselves that which they send forth, and so come in contact with people similar to themselves. The old adage "Birds of a feather flock together" has a deeper significance than is generally attached to it, for in the thought-world as in the world of matter, each clings to its kind.

Do you wish for kindness? Be kind.
Do you ask for truth? Be true.
What you give of yourself you find;
Your world is a reflex of you.

If you are one of those who are praying for, and looking forward to, a happier world beyond the grave, here is a message of gladness for you: you may enter into and realize that happy world now; it fills the whole universe, and it is within you, waiting for you to find, acknowledge, and possess. Said one who knew the inner laws of Being, "When men shall say lo here, or lo there, go not after them; the kingdom of God is within you." What you have to do is to believe this, simply believe it with a mind unshadowed by doubt, and then meditate upon it till you understand it. You will then begin to purify and to build your inner world, and as you proceed, passing from revelation to revelation, from realization to realization, you will discover the utter powerlessness of outward things beside the magic potency of a self-governed soul.

If thou would'st right the world,
And banish all its evils and its woes,
    Make its wild places bloom,
And its drear deserts blossom as the rose,—
    Then right thyself.

If thou would'st turn the world
From its long, lone captivity in sin.
    Restore all broken hearts,
Slay grief, and let sweet consolation in,—
    Turn thou thyself.

If thou would'st cure the world
Of its long sickness, end its grief and pain;
    Bring in all-healing Joy,
And give to the afflicted rest again,—
    Then cure thyself.

If thou would'st wake the world
Out of its dream of death and dark'ning strife,
    Bring it to Love and Peace,
And Light and brightness of immortal Life,—
    Wake thou thyself.

II
"The 'Original Simplicity'"

—◆◆◇❋◇◆◆—

(from *All These Things Added*, 1903)

This piece highlights the influence that Allen took from Taoism and Buddhism. Allen ranks as one of the first popular inspirational writers who emphasized Eastern religious wisdom. In our time, the words "simplicity" and "simple living" are marketing tropes. For Allen, as with Thoreau a generation earlier, these concepts emerged from the depths of perennial tradition.

—MH

The "Original Simplicity"

Life is simple. Being is simple. The universe is simple. Complexity arises in ignorance and self-delusion. The "Original Simplicity" of Lao-tze is a term expressive of the universe as it *is*, and not as it *appears*. Looking through the woven network of his own illusions, man sees interminable complication and unfathomable mystery, and so loses himself in the labyrinths of his own making. Let a man put away egotism, and he will see the universe in all the beauty of its pristine simplicity. Let him annihilate the delusion of the personal "I," and he will destroy all the illusions which spring from that "I." He will thus "re-become a little child," and will "revert to Original Simplicity."

When a man succeeds in entirely forgetting (annihilating) his personal self, he becomes a mirror in which the universal Reality is faultlessly reflected. He is awakened, and henceforward he lives, not in dreams, but realities.

Pythagoras saw the universe in the ten numbers, but even this simplicity may be further reduced, and the universe ultimately be found to be contained in the number ONE, for all the numerals and all their Infinite complications are but additions of the *One*.

Let life cease to be lived as a fragmentary thing, and let it be lived as a perfect Whole; the simplicity of the Perfect will then be revealed. How shall the fragment comprehend the Whole? Yet how simple that the Whole should comprehend the fragment. How shall sin perceive Holiness? Yet how plain that Holiness should understand sin. He who would become the Greater let him abandon the lesser. In no form is the circle contained, but in the circle all forms are contained. In no color is the radiant light imprisoned, but in the radiant light all colors are embodied. Let a man destroy all the forms of self, and he shall apprehend the Circle of Perfection; let him submerge, in the silent depths of his being, the varying colors of his thoughts and desires, and he shall be illuminated with the White Light of Divine Knowledge. In the perfect chord of music the single note, though forgotten, is indispensably contained, and the drop of water becomes of supreme usefulness by losing itself in the ocean. Sink thyself compassionately in the heart of humanity, and thou shalt reproduce the harmonies of Heaven; lose thyself in unlimited love toward all, and thou shalt work enduring works and shalt become one with the eternal Ocean of Bliss.

Man evolves outward to the periphery of complexity, and then involves backward to the Central Simplicity. When a man discovers that it is mathematically impossible for him to know the universe before knowing himself, he then starts upon the Way which leads to the Original Simplicity. He begins to unfold from within, and as he unfolds himself, he enfolds the universe.

Cease to speculate about God, and find the all-embracing Good within thee, then shalt thou see the emptiness and vanity of speculation, knowing thyself one with God.

He who will not give up his secret lust, his covetousness, his anger, his opinion about this or that can see nor know nothing; he will remain a dullard in the school of Wisdom, though he be accounted learned in the colleges.

If a man would find the Key of Knowledge, let him find himself. Thy sins are not thyself; they are not any part of thyself; they are diseases which thou hast come to love. Cease to cling to them, and they will no longer cling to thee. Let them fall away, and thy self shall stand revealed. Thou shalt then know thyself as Comprehensive Vision, Invincible Principle, Immortal Life, and eternal Good.

The impure man believes impurity to be his rightful condition, but the pure man knows himself as pure being; he also, penetrating the Veils, sees all others as pure being. Purity is extremely simple, and needs no argument to support it; impurity is interminably complex, and is ever involved in defensive argument. Truth *lives* itself. A blameless life is the only witness of Truth. Men cannot see, and will not accept the witness until they find it within themselves; and having found it, a man becomes silent before his fellows. Truth is so simple that it cannot be found in the region of argument and advertisement, and so silent that it is only manifested in actions.

So extremely simple is Original Simplicity that a man must let go his hold of everything before he can perceive it. The great arch is strong by virtue of the hollowness underneath, and a wise man becomes strong and invincible by emptying himself.

Meekness, Patience, Love, Compassion, and Wisdom— these are the dominant qualities of Original Simplicity; therefore the imperfect cannot understand it. Wisdom only can apprehend Wisdom; therefore the fool says, "No man is wise." The imperfect man says, "No man can be perfect," and he therefore remains where he is. Though he live with a perfect man all his life, he shall not behold his perfection. Meekness he will call cowardice; Patience, Love, and Compassion he will see as weakness; and Wisdom will appear to him as folly. Faultless discrimination belongs to the Perfect Whole, and resides not in any part; therefore men are exhorted to refrain from judgment until they have themselves manifested the Perfect Life.

Arriving at Original Simplicity, opacity disappears, and the universal transparency becomes apparent. He who has found the indwelling Reality of his own being has found the original and universal Reality. Knowing the Divine Heart within, all hearts are known, and the thoughts of all men become his who has become the master of his own thoughts; therefore the good man does not defend himself, but molds the minds of others to his own likeness.

As the problematical transcends crudity, so Pure Goodness transcends the problematical. All problems vanish when Pure Goodness is reached; therefore the good man is called

"The slayer of illusions." What problem can vex where sin is not? O thou who strivest loudly and restest not! Retire into the holy silence of thine own being, and live therefrom. So shalt thou, finding Pure Goodness, rend in twain the Veil of the Temple of Illusion, and shalt enter into the Patience, Peace, and transcendent Glory of the Perfect, for Pure Goodness and Original Simplicity are one.

III
"The Might of Meekness"

+❧❊❧+

(from *All These Things Added*, 1903)

In this piece, Allen combines Taoist and Eastern thought to illuminate Christ's celebration of the meek. Meekness, in Allen's teaching, is a kind of stoic detachment from worldly frictions and a willingness to be overcome by the machinations of men—because the truly meek person understands that his strength emanates from unseen sources. To be meek is to cease fighting and struggling over ephemera, so that true beingness can enter you. —MH

The Might
of Meekness

The mountain bends not to the fiercest storm, but it shields the fledgling and the lamb; and though all men tread upon it, yet it protects them, and bears them up upon its deathless bosom. Even so is it with the meek man who, though shaken and disturbed by none, yet compassionately bends to shield the lowliest creature, and, though he may be despised, lifts all men up, and lovingly protects them.

As glorious as the mountain in its silent might is the divine man in his silent Meekness; like its form, his loving compassion is expansive and sublime. Truly his body, like the mountain's base, is fixed in the valleys and the mists; but the summit of his being is eternally bathed in cloudless glory, and lives with the Silences.

He who has found Meekness has found divinity; he has realized the divine consciousness, and knows himself as divine. He also knows all others as divine, though they know it not themselves, being asleep and dreaming. Meekness is a divine quality, and as such is all-powerful. The meek man overcomes by not resisting, and by allowing himself to be defeated he attains to the Supreme Conquest.

The man who conquers another by force is strong; the man who conquers himself by Meekness is mighty. He who conquers another by force will himself likewise be conquered; he who conquers himself by Meekness will never be overthrown, for the human cannot overcome the divine. The meek man is triumphant in defeat. Socrates lives the more by being put to death; in the crucified Jesus the risen Christ is revealed, and Stephen in receiving his stoning defies the hurting power of stones. That which is real cannot be destroyed, but only that which is unreal. When a man finds that within him which is real, which is constant, abiding, changeless, and eternal, he enters into that Reality, and becomes meek. All the powers of darkness will come against him, but they will do him no hurt, and will at last depart from him.

The meek man is found in the time of trial; when other men fall he stands. His patience is not destroyed by the foolish passions of others, and when they come against him he does not "strive nor cry." He knows the utter powerlessness of all evil, having overcome it in himself, and lives in the changeless strength and power of divine Good.

Meekness is one aspect of the operation of that changeless Love which is at the Heart of all things, and is therefore an imperishable quality. He who lives in it is without fear, knowing the Highest, and having the lowest under his feet.

The meek man shines in darkness, and flourishes in obscurity. Meekness cannot boast, nor advertise itself, nor thrive on popularity. It is *practiced*, and is seen or not seen; being a spiritual quality it is perceived only by the eye of the spirit. Those who are not spiritually awakened see it not, nor do they love it, being enamored of, and blinded by, worldly shows and appearances. Nor does history take note of the meek man. Its glory is that of strife and self-aggrandizement; his is the glory of peace and gentleness. History chronicles the earthly, not the heavenly acts. Yet though he lives in obscurity he cannot be hidden (how can light be hid?); he continues to shine after he has withdrawn himself from the world, and is worshiped by the world which knew him not.

That the meek man should be neglected, abused, or misunderstood is reckoned by him as of no account, and therefore not to be considered, much less resisted. He knows that all such weapons are the flimsiest and most ineffectual of shadows. To them, therefore, who give him evil he gives good. He resists none, and thereby conquers all.

He who imagines he can be injured by others, and who seeks to justify and defend himself against them, does not understand Meekness, does not comprehend the essence and meaning of life. "He abused me, he beat me, he defeated me, he robbed me. In those who harbor such thoughts hatred will never cease . . . for hatred ceases not by hatred at any time; hatred ceases by love." What sayest thou, thy neighbor has spoken of thee falsely? Well, what of that? Can a falsity hurt thee? That which is false is false, and there is an end of it. It is without life, and without power to hurt any but him who seeks to hurt by it. It is nothing to thee that thy neighbor should speak falsely of thee, but it is much to thee that thou shouldst resist him, and seek to justify thyself, for, by so doing, thou givest life and vitality to thy neighbor's falseness, so that thou art injured and distressed. Take all evil out of thine own heart, then shalt thou see the folly of resisting it in another. Thou wilt be trodden on? Thou art trodden on already if thou thinkest thus. The injury that thou seest as coming from another comes only from thyself. The wrong thought, or word, or act of another has no power to hurt thee unless thou galvanize it into life by thy passionate resistance, and so receivest it into thyself. If any man slander me, that is his concern, not mine. I have to do with my own soul, not with my neighbor's. Though all the world misjudge me, it is no business of mine; but that I should possess my soul in Purity and Love, that is all my business. There shall be no end to strife until men cease to justify themselves. He who would have wars cease let him cease to defend any party—let him cease to defend himself. Not by strife can peace come, but by ceasing from strife. The glory of Caesar resides in the resistance of his enemies. They resist and fall. Give to Caesar that which Caesar demands, and Caesar's glory and power are gone. Thus, by submission does the meek man conquer the strong man; but it is not that outward show of submission which is slavery, it is that inward and spiritual submission which is *freedom*.

Claiming no *rights*, the meek man is not troubled with self-defense and self-justification; he lives in love, and therefore comes under the immediate and vital protection of the

Great Love which is the Eternal Law of the universe. He neither claims nor seeks his own; thus do all things come to him, and all the universe shields and protects him.

He who says, "I have tried Meekness, and it has failed" has not tried Meekness. It cannot be tried as an experiment. It is only arrived at by unreserved self-sacrifice. Meekness does not consist merely in non-resistance in action; it consists preeminently in non-resistance in *thought*, in ceasing to hold or to have any selfish, condemnatory, or retaliatory thoughts. The meek man, therefore, cannot "take offense" or have his "feelings hurt," living above hatred, folly, and vanity. Meekness can never fail.

O thou who searchest for the Heavenly Life! Strive after Meekness; increase thy patience and forbearance day by day; bid thy tongue cease from all harsh words; withdraw thy mind from selfish arguments, and refuse to brood upon thy wrongs; so living, thou shalt carefully tend and cultivate the pure and delicate flower of Meekness in thy heart, until at last, its divine sweetness and purity and beauteous perfection shall be revealed to thee, and thou shalt become gentle, joyful, and strong. Repine not that thou art surrounded by irritable and selfish people; but rather rejoice that thou art so favored as to have thine own imperfections revealed to thee, and that thou art so placed as to necessitate within thee a constant struggle for self-mastery and the attainment of perfection. The more there is of harshness and selfishness around thee, the greater is the need of thy Meekness and love. If others seek to wrong thee, all the more is it needful that thou shouldst cease from all wrong, and live in love; if others preach Meekness, humility, and love, and do not practice these, trouble not, nor be annoyed; but do thou, in the silence of thy heart, and in thy contact with others, *practice* these things, and they shall preach themselves. And though thou utter no declamatory word, and stand before no gathered audience, thou shalt teach the whole world. As thou becomest meek, thou shalt learn the deepest secrets of the universe. Nothing is hidden from him who overcomes himself. Into the cause of causes shalt thou penetrate, and lifting, one after another, every veil of illusion, shalt reach at last the inmost Heart of Being. Thus becoming one with Life, thou shalt know all life, and, seeing into causes, and knowing realities, thou shalt be no more anxious about thyself, and others, and the world, but shalt see that all things that are are engines of the Great Law. Canopied with gentleness, thou shalt bless where others curse; love where others hate; forgive where others condemn; yield where others strive; give up where others grasp; lose where others gain. And in their strength they shall be weak; and in thy weakness thou shalt be strong; yea, thou shalt mightily prevail. He that hath not unbroken gentleness hath not Truth:

> *Therefore when Heaven would save a man, it enfolds him*
> *with gentleness.*

IV
As a Man Thinketh

(complete text, 1903)

Here is the classic meditation that made the proverbial phrase "as a man thinketh" into the informal motto of the New Thought, motivational, and self-help movements in the new century. Probably no single work of modern inspiration has been as influential or as widely echoed. The triumph of this single, beautiful volume brought Allen worldwide readership and authorial posterity. Written early in Allen's career, As a Man Thinketh *has become a standard work for spiritual readers of every background and tradition. It is an inlet of the perennial philosophy. Read in the right moment, at the right time, and in the right spirit,* As a Man Thinketh *work can reorganize your focus, priorities, and sense of self.* —MH

Foreword

This little volume (the result of meditation and experience) is not intended as an exhaustive treatise on the much-written-upon subject of the power of thought. It is suggestive rather than explanatory, its object being to stimulate men and women to the discovery and perception of the truth that—

They themselves are makers of themselves

by virtue of the thoughts which they choose and encourage; that mind is the master weaver, both of the inner garment of character and the outer garment of circumstance, and that, as they may have hitherto woven in ignorance and pain they may now weave in enlightenment and happiness.

—James Allen

Broad Park Avenue, Ilfracombe, England

Thought and Character

The aphorism "As a man thinketh in his heart so is he" not only embraces the whole of a man's being, but is so comprehensive as to reach out to every condition and circumstance of his life. A man is literally *what he thinks*, his character being the complete sum of all his thoughts.

As the plant springs from, and could not be without, the seed, so every act of a man springs from the hidden seeds of thought, and could not have appeared without them. This applies equally to those acts called "spontaneous" and "unpremeditated" as to those which are deliberately executed.

Act is the blossom of thought, and joy and suffering are its fruits; thus does a man garner in the sweet and bitter fruitage of his own husbandry.

> *Thought in the mind hath made us. What we are*
> *By thought was wrought and built. If a man's mind*

Hath evil thoughts, pain comes on him as comes
The wheel the ox behind. . . .

                                        . . . If one endure

In purity of thought, joy follows him
As his own shadow—sure.

Man is a growth by law, and not a creation by artifice, and cause and effect is as absolute and undeviating in the hidden realm of thought as in the world of visible and material things. A noble and Godlike character is not a thing of favor or chance, but is the natural result of continued effort in right thinking, the effect of long-cherished association with Godlike thoughts. An ignoble and bestial character, by the same process, is the result of the continued harboring of groveling thoughts.

Man is made or unmade by himself; in the armory of thought he forges the weapons by which he destroys himself; he also fashions the tools with which he builds for himself heavenly mansions of joy and strength and peace. By the right choice and true application of thought, man ascends to the Divine Perfection; by the abuse and wrong application of thought, he descends below the level of the beast. Between these two extremes are all the grades of character, and man is their maker and master.

Of all the beautiful truths pertaining to the soul which have been restored and brought to light in this age, none is more gladdening or fruitful of divine promise and confidence than this—that man is the master of thought, the molder of character, and the maker and shaper of condition, environment, and destiny.

As a being of Power, Intelligence, and Love, and the lord of his own thoughts, man holds the key to every situation, and contains within himself that transforming and regenerative agency by which he may make himself what he wills.

Man is always the master, even in his weakest and most abandoned state; but in his weakness and degradation he is the foolish master who misgoverns his "household." When he begins to reflect upon his condition, and to search diligently for the Law upon which his being is established, he then becomes the wise master, directing his energies with intelligence, and fashioning his thoughts to fruitful issues. Such is the *conscious* master, and man can only thus become by discovering *within himself the* laws of thought; which discovery is totally a matter of application, self-analysis, and experience.

Only by much searching and mining are gold and diamonds obtained, and man can find every truth connected with his being if he will dig deep into the mine of his soul; and that he is the maker of his character, the molder of his life, and the builder of his destiny, he may unerringly prove, if he will watch, control, and alter his thoughts, tracing their effects upon himself, upon others, and upon his life and circumstances, linking cause and effect by patient practice and investigation, and utilizing his every experience, even to the most trivial, everyday occurrence, as a means of obtaining that knowledge of himself which is Understanding, Wisdom,

Power. In this direction, as in no other, is the law absolute that "He that seeketh findeth; and to him that knocketh it shall be opened"; for only by patience, practice, and ceaseless importunity can a man enter the Door of the Temple of Knowledge.

Effect of Thought on Circumstances

A man's mind may be likened to a garden, which may be intelligently cultivated or allowed to run wild; but whether cultivated or neglected, it must, and will, *bring forth*. If no useful seeds are *put* into it, then an abundance of useless weed seeds will *fall* therein, and will continue to produce their kind.

Just as a gardener cultivates his plot, keeping it free from weeds, and growing the flowers and fruits which he requires, so may a man tend the garden of his mind, weeding out all the wrong, useless, and impure thoughts, and cultivating toward perfection the flowers and fruits of right, useful, and pure thoughts. By pursuing this process, a man sooner or later discovers that he is the master gardener of his soul, the director of his life. He also reveals, within himself, the laws of thought, and understands, with ever-increasing accuracy, how the thought forces and mind elements operate in the shaping of his character, circumstances, and destiny.

Thought and character are one, and as character can only manifest and discover itself through environment and circumstance, the outer conditions of a person's life will always be found to be harmoniously related to his inner state. This does not mean that a man's circumstances at any given time are an indication of his *entire* character, but that those circumstances are so intimately connected with some vital thought element within himself that, for the time being, they are indispensable to his development.

Every man is where he is by the law of his being; the thoughts which he has built into his character have brought him there, and in the arrangement of his life there is no element of chance, but all is the result of a law which cannot err. This is just as true of those who feel "out of harmony" with their surroundings as of those who are contented with them.

As a progressive and evolving being, man is where he is that he may learn that he may grow; and as he learns the spiritual lesson which any circumstance contains for him, it passes away and gives place to other circumstances.

Man is buffeted by circumstances so long as he believes himself to be the creature of outside conditions, but when he realizes that he is a creative power, and that he may command the hidden soil and seeds of his being out of which circumstances grow, he then becomes the rightful master of himself.

That circumstances *grow* out of thought every man knows who has for any length of time practiced self-control and self-purification, for he will have noticed that the alteration in his circumstances has been in exact ratio with his altered mental condition. So true is this that when a man earnestly applies himself to remedy the defects in his character, and makes swift and marked progress, he passes rapidly through a succession of vicissitudes.

The soul attracts that which it secretly harbors; that which it loves, and also that which it fears; it reaches the height of its cherished aspirations; it falls to the level of its unchastened desires—and circumstances are the means by which the soul receives its own.

Every thought seed sown or allowed to fall into the mind, and to take root there, produces its own, blossoming sooner or later into act, and bearing its own fruitage of opportunity and circumstance. Good thoughts bear good fruit, bad thoughts bad fruit.

The outer world of circumstance shapes itself to the inner world of thought, and both pleasant and unpleasant external conditions are factors which make for the ultimate good of the individual. As the reaper of his own harvest, man learns both by suffering and bliss.

Following the inmost desires, aspirations, thoughts, by which he allows himself to be dominated (pursuing the will-o'-the-wisps of impure imaginings or steadfastly walking the highway of strong and high endeavor), a man at last arrives at their fruition and fulfillment in the outer conditions of his life. The laws of growth and adjustment everywhere obtain.

A man does not come to the almshouse or the jail by the tyranny of fate or circumstance, but by the pathway of groveling thoughts and base desires. Nor does a pure-minded man fall suddenly into crime by stress of any mere external force; the criminal thought had long been secretly fostered in the heart, and the hour of opportunity revealed its gathered power. Circumstance does not make the man; it reveals him to himself. No such conditions can exist as descending into vice and its attendant sufferings apart from vicious inclinations, or ascending into virtue and its pure happiness without the continued cultivation of virtuous aspirations; and man, therefore, as the lord and master of thought, is the maker of himself, the shaper and author of environment. Even at birth the soul comes to its own, and through every step of its earthly pilgrimage it attracts those combinations of conditions which reveal itself, which are the reflections of its own purity and impurity, its strength and weakness.

Men do not attract that which they *want*, but that which they *are*. Their whims, fancies, and ambitions are thwarted at every step, but their inmost thoughts and desires are fed with their own food, be it foul or clean. The "divinity that shapes our ends" is in ourselves; it is our very self. Man is manacled only by himself: thought and action are the jailers of Fate—they imprison, being base; they are also the angels of Freedom—they liberate, being noble. Not what he wishes and prays for does a man get, but what he justly earns. His wishes and prayers are only gratified and answered when they harmonize with his thoughts and actions.

In the light of this truth, what, then, is the meaning of "fighting against circumstances"? It means that a man is continually revolting against an *effect* without, while all the time he is nourishing and preserving its *cause* in his heart. That cause may take the form of a conscious vice or an unconscious weakness; but whatever it is, it stubbornly retards the efforts of its possessor, and thus calls aloud for remedy.

Men are anxious to improve their circumstances, but are unwilling to improve themselves; they therefore remain bound. The man who does not shrink from self-crucifixion can never fail to accomplish the object upon which his heart is set. This is as true of earthly as of heavenly things. Even the man whose sole object is to acquire wealth must be prepared to make great personal sacrifices before he can accomplish his object; and how much more so he who would realize a strong and well-poised life?

Here is a man who is wretchedly poor. He is extremely anxious that his surroundings and home comforts should be improved, yet all the time he shirks his work, and considers he is justified in trying to deceive his employer on the ground of the insufficiency of his wages. Such a man does not understand the simplest rudiments of those principles which are the basis of true prosperity, and is not only totally unfitted to rise out of his wretchedness, but is actually attracting to himself a still deeper wretchedness by dwelling in, and acting out, indolent, deceptive, and unmanly thoughts.

Here is a rich man who is the victim of a painful and persistent disease as the result of gluttony. He is willing to give large sums of money to get rid of it, but he will not sacrifice his gluttonous desires.

He wants to gratify his taste for rich and unnatural viands and have his health as well. Such a man is totally unfit to have health, because he has not yet learned the first principles of a healthy life.

Here is an employer of labor who adopts crooked measures to avoid paying the regulation wage, and, in the hope of making larger profits, reduces the wages of his workpeople. Such a man is altogether unfitted for prosperity, and when he finds himself bankrupt, both as regards reputation and riches, he blames circumstances, not knowing that he is the sole author of his condition.

I have introduced these three cases merely as illustrative of the truth that man is the causer (though nearly always unconsciously) of his circumstances, and that, while aiming at a good end, he is continually frustrating its accomplishment by encouraging thoughts and desires which cannot possibly harmonize with that end. Such cases could be multiplied and varied almost indefinitely, but this is not necessary, as the reader can, if he so resolves, trace the action of the laws of thought in his own mind and life, and until this is done, mere external facts cannot serve as a ground of reasoning.

Circumstances, however, are so complicated, thought is so deeply rooted, and the conditions of happiness vary so vastly with individuals that a man's *entire* soul condition (although it may be known to himself) cannot be judged by another from the external aspect of his life alone. A man may be honest in certain directions, yet suffer privations; a man may be dishonest in certain directions, yet acquire wealth; but the conclusion usually formed that the one man fails *because of his particular honesty*, and that the other prospers *because of his particular dishonesty*, is the result of a superficial judgment, which assumes that the dishonest man is almost totally corrupt, and the honest man almost entirely virtuous. In the light of a deeper knowledge and wider experience, such judgment is found to be erroneous. The dishonest man may have some admirable virtues which the other does not possess; and the honest man obnoxious vices which are absent in the other. The honest man reaps the good results of his honest thoughts and acts; he also brings upon himself the sufferings which his vices produce. The dishonest man likewise garners his own suffering and happiness.

It is pleasing to human vanity to believe that one suffers because of one's virtue; but not until a man has extirpated every sickly, bitter, and impure thought from his mind, and washed every sinful stain from his soul, can he be in a position to know and declare that his sufferings are the result of his good, and not of his bad qualities; and on the way to, yet long before he has reached, that supreme perfection, he will have found, working in his mind and life, the Great Law which is absolutely just, and which cannot, therefore, give good for evil, evil for good. Possessed of such knowledge, he will then know, looking back upon his past ignorance and blindness, that his life is, and always was, justly ordered, and that all his past experiences, good and bad, were the equitable outworking of his evolving, yet unevolved self.

Good thoughts and actions can never produce bad results; bad thoughts and actions can never produce good results.

This is but saying that nothing can come from corn but corn, nothing from nettles but nettles. Men understand this law in the natural world, and work with it; but few understand it in the mental and moral world (though its operation there is just as simple and undeviating), and they, therefore, do not cooperate with it.

Suffering is *always* the effect of wrong thought in some direction. It is an indication that the individual is out of harmony with himself, with the Law of his being. The sole and supreme use of suffering is to purify, to burn out all that is useless and impure. Suffering ceases for him who is pure. There could be no object in burning gold after the dross had been removed, and a perfectly pure and enlightened being could not suffer.

The circumstances which a man encounters with suffering are the result of his own mental inharmony. The circumstances which a man encounters with blessedness are the result of his own mental harmony. Blessedness, not material possessions, is the measure of right thought; wretchedness, not lack of material possessions, is the measure of wrong thought. A man may be cursed and rich; he may be blessed and poor. Blessedness and riches are only joined together when the riches are rightly and wisely used; and the poor man only descends into wretchedness when he regards his lot as a burden unjustly imposed.

Indigence and indulgence are the two extremes of wretchedness. They are both equally unnatural and the result of mental disorder. A man is not rightly conditioned until he is a happy, healthy, and prosperous being; and happiness, health, and prosperity are the result of a harmonious adjustment of the inner with the outer, of the man with his surroundings.

A man only begins to be a man when he ceases to whine and revile, and commences to search for the hidden justice which regulates his life. And as he adapts his mind to that regulating factor, he ceases to accuse others as the cause of his condition, and builds himself up in strong and noble thoughts; ceases to kick against circumstances, but begins to use them as aids to his more rapid progress, and as a means of discovering the hidden powers and possibilities within himself.

Law, not confusion, is the dominating principle in the universe; justice, not injustice, is the soul and substance of life; and righteousness, not corruption, is the molding and moving force in the spiritual government of the world. This being so, man has but to right himself to find that the universe is right; and during the process of putting himself right, he will find that as he alters his thoughts toward things, and other people, things and other people will alter toward him.

The proof of this truth is in every person, and it therefore admits of easy investigation by systematic introspection and self-analysis. Let a man radically alter his thoughts, and he will be astonished at the rapid transformation it will effect in the material conditions of his life. Men imagine that thought can be kept secret, but it cannot; it rapidly crystallizes into habit, and habit solidifies into circumstance. Bestial thoughts crystallize into habits of drunkenness and sensuality, which solidify into circumstances of destitution and disease; impure thoughts of every kind crystallize into enervating and confusing habits, which solidify into distracting and adverse circumstances; thoughts of fear, doubt, and indecision crystallize into weak, unmanly, and irresolute habits, which solidify into circumstances of failure, indigence, and slavish dependence; lazy thoughts crystallize into habits of uncleanliness and dishonesty, which solidify into circumstances of foulness and beggary; hateful and condemnatory thoughts crystallize into habits of accusation and violence, which solidify into circumstances of injury and persecution; selfish thoughts of all kinds crystallize into habits of self-seeking, which solidify into circumstances more or less distressing. On the other hand, beautiful thoughts of all kinds crystallize into habits of grace and kindliness, which solidify into genial and sunny circumstances; pure thoughts crystallize into habits of temperance and self-control, which solidify into circumstances of repose and peace; thoughts of courage, self-reliance, and decision crystallize into manly habits, which solidify into circumstances of success, plenty, and freedom; energetic thoughts crystallize into habits of cleanliness and industry, which solidify into circumstances of pleasantness; gentle and forgiving thoughts crystallize into habits of gentleness, which solidify into protective and preservative circumstances; loving and unselfish thoughts crystallize into habits of self-forgetfulness for others, which solidify into circumstances of sure and abiding prosperity and true riches.

A particular train of thought persisted in, be it good or bad, cannot fail to produce its results on the character and circumstances. A man cannot *directly* choose his circumstances, but he can choose his thoughts, and so indirectly, yet surely, shape his circumstances.

Nature helps every man to the gratification of the thoughts which he most encourages, and opportunities are presented which will most speedily bring to the surface both the good and evil thoughts.

Let a man cease from his sinful thoughts, and all the world will soften toward him, and be ready to help him; let him put away his weakly and sickly thoughts, and lo! opportunities will spring up on every hand to aid his strong resolves; let him encourage good thoughts, and no hard fate shall bind him down to wretchedness and shame. The world is your kaleidoscope, and the varying combinations of colors which at every succeeding moment it presents to you are the exquisitely adjusted pictures of your ever-moving thoughts.

> *You will be what you will to be;*
> *Let failure find its false content*
> *In that poor word, "environment,"*
> *But spirit scorns it, and is free.*
>
> *It masters time, it conquers space;*
> *It cows that boastful trickster, Chance,*
> *And bids the tyrant Circumstance*
> *Uncrown, and fill a servant's place.*
>
> *The human Will, that force unseen,*
> *The offspring of a deathless Soul,*
> *Can hew a way to any goal,*
> *Though walls of granite intervene.*

Be not impatient in delay,
But wait as one who understands;
When spirit rises and commands,
The gods are ready to obey.

Effect of Thought on Health and the Body

The body is the servant of the mind. It obeys the operations of the mind, whether they be deliberately chosen or automatically expressed. At the bidding of unlawful thoughts the body sinks rapidly into disease and decay; at the command of glad and beautiful thoughts it becomes clothed with youthfulness and beauty.

Disease and health, like circumstances, are rooted in thought. Sickly thoughts will express themselves through a sickly body. Thoughts of fear have been known to kill a man as speedily as a bullet, and they are continually killing thousands of people just as surely though less rapidly. The people who live in fear of disease are the people who get it. Anxiety quickly demoralizes the whole body, and lays it open to the entrance of disease; while impure thoughts, even if not physically indulged, will soon shatter the nervous system.

Strong, pure, and happy thoughts build up the body in vigor and grace. The body is a delicate and plastic instrument, which responds readily to the thoughts by which it is impressed, and habits of thought will produce their own effects, good or bad, upon it.

Men will continue to have impure and poisoned blood so long as they propagate unclean thoughts. Out of a clean heart comes a clean life and a clean body. Out of a defiled mind proceeds a defiled life and a corrupt body. Thought is the font of action, life, and manifestation; make the fountain pure, and all will be pure.

Change of diet will not help a man who will not change his thoughts. When a man makes his thoughts pure, he no longer desires impure food.

Clean thoughts make clean habits. The so-called saint who does not wash his body is not a saint. He who has strengthened and purified his thoughts does not need to consider the malevolent microbe.

If you would perfect your body, guard your mind. If you would renew your body, beautify your mind. Thoughts of malice, envy, disappointment, despondency rob the body of its health and grace. A sour face does not come by chance; it is made by sour thoughts. Wrinkles that mar are drawn by folly, passion, pride.

I know a woman of ninety-six who has the bright, innocent face of a girl. I know a man well under middle age whose face is drawn into inharmonious contours. The one is the result of a sweet and sunny disposition; the other is the outcome of passion and discontent.

As you cannot have a sweet and wholesome abode unless you admit the air and sunshine freely into your rooms, so a strong body and a bright, happy, or serene countenance can only result from the free admittance into the mind of thoughts of joy and good will and serenity.

On the faces of the aged there are wrinkles made by sympathy; others by strong and pure thought; and others are carved by passion: who cannot distinguish them? With those who have lived righteously, age is calm, peaceful, and softly mellowed, like the setting sun. I have recently seen a philosopher on his deathbed. He was not old except in years. He died as sweetly and peacefully as he had lived.

There is no physician like cheerful thought for dissipating the ills of the body; there is no comforter to compare with good will for dispersing the shadows of grief and sorrow. To live continually in thoughts of ill will, cynicism, suspicion, and envy is to be Confined in a self-made prison hole. But to think well of all, to be cheerful with all, to patiently learn to find the good in all—such unselfish thoughts are the very portals of heaven; and to dwell day by day in thoughts of peace toward every creature will bring abounding peace to their possessor.

Thought and Purpose

Until thought is linked with purpose there is no intelligent accomplishment. With the majority the bark of thought is allowed to "drift" upon the ocean of life. Aimlessness is a vice, and such drifting must not continue for him who would steer clear of catastrophe and destruction.

They who have no central purpose in their life fall an easy prey to petty worries, fears, troubles, and self-pityings, all of which are indications of weakness, which lead, just as surely as deliberately planned sins (though by a different route), to failure, unhappiness, and loss, for weakness cannot persist in a power-evolving universe.

A man should conceive of a legitimate purpose in his heart, and set out to accomplish it. He should make this purpose the centralizing point of his thoughts. It may take the form of a spiritual ideal, or it may be a worldly object, according to his nature at the time being; but whichever it is, he should steadily focus his thought forces upon the object which he has set before him. He should make this purpose his supreme duty, and should devote himself to its attainment, not allowing his thoughts to wander away into ephemeral fancies, longings, and imaginings. This is the royal road to self-control and true concentration of thought. Even if he fails again and again to accomplish his purpose (as he necessarily must until weakness is overcome), the *strength of character gained* will be the measure of his *true* success, and this will form a new starting point for future power and triumph.

Those who are not prepared for the apprehension of a *great* purpose should fix their thoughts upon the faultless performance of their duty, no matter how insignificant their task may appear. Only in this way can the thoughts be gathered and focused, and resolution and energy be developed, which being done, there is nothing which may not be accomplished.

The weakest soul, knowing its own weakness, and believing this truth—*that strength can only be developed by effort and practice*—will, thus believing, at once begin to exert itself, and, adding effort to effort, patience to patience, and strength to strength, will never cease to develop, and will at last grow divinely strong.

As the physically weak man can make himself strong by careful and patient training, so the man of weak thoughts can make them strong by exercising himself in right thinking.

To put away aimlessness and weakness, and to begin to think with purpose, is to enter the ranks of those strong ones who only recognize failure as one of the pathways to attainment; who make all conditions serve them, and who think strongly, attempt fearlessly, and accomplish masterfully.

Having conceived of his purpose, a man should mentally mark out a *straight* pathway to its achievement, looking neither to the right nor the left. Doubts and fears should be rigorously excluded; they are disintegrating elements which break up the straight line of effort, rendering it crooked, ineffectual, useless. Thoughts of doubt and fear never accomplish anything, and never can. They always lead to failure. Purpose, energy, power to do, and all strong thoughts cease when doubt and fear creep in.

The will to do springs from the knowledge that we *can* do. Doubt and fear are the great enemies of knowledge, and he who encourages them, who does not slay them, thwarts himself at every step.

He who has conquered doubt and fear has conquered failure. His every thought is allied with power, and all difficulties are bravely met and wisely overcome. His purposes are seasonably planted, and they bloom and bring forth fruit which does not fall prematurely to the ground.

Thought allied fearlessly to purpose becomes creative force: he who *knows* this is ready to become something higher and stronger than a mere bundle of wavering thoughts and fluctuating sensations; he who does this has become the conscious and intelligent wielder of his mental powers.

The Thought-Factor
In Achievement

All that a man achieves and all that he fails to achieve is the direct result of his own thoughts. In a justly ordered universe, where loss of equipoise would mean total destruction, individual responsibility must be absolute. A man's weakness and strength, purity and impurity, are his own, and not another man's; they are brought about by himself, and not by another; and they can only be altered by himself, never by another. His condition is also his own, and not another man's. His suffering and his happiness are evolved from within. As he thinks, so he is; as he continues to think, so he remains.

A strong man cannot help a weaker unless that weaker is *willing* to be helped, and even then the weak man must become strong of himself; he must, by his own efforts, develop the strength which he admires in another. None but himself can alter his condition.

It has been usual for men to think and to say, "Many men are slaves because one is an oppressor; let us hate the oppressor." Now, however, there is among an increasing few a tendency to reverse this judgment, and to say, "One man is an oppressor because many are slaves; let us despise the slaves." The truth is that oppressor and slave are cooperators in ignorance, and, while seeming to afflict each other, are in reality afflicting themselves. A perfect Knowledge perceives the action of law in the weakness of the oppressed and the misapplied power of the oppressor; a perfect Love, seeing the suffering which both states entail, condemns neither; a perfect Compassion embraces both oppressor and oppressed.

He who has conquered weakness, and has put away all selfish thoughts, belongs neither to oppressor nor oppressed. He is free.

A man can only rise, conquer, and achieve by lifting up his thoughts. He can only remain weak, abject, and miserable by refusing to lift up his thoughts.

Before a man can achieve anything, even in worldly things, he must lift his thoughts above slavish animal indulgence. He may not, in order to succeed, give up *all* animality and selfishness, by any means; but a portion of it must, at least, be sacrificed. A man whose first thought is bestial indulgence could neither think clearly nor plan methodically; he could not find and develop his latent resources, and would fail in any undertaking. Not having commenced manfully to control his thoughts, he is not in a position to control affairs and to adopt serious responsibilities. He is not fit to act independently and stand alone. But he is limited only by the thoughts which he chooses.

There can be no progress, no achievement without sacrifice, and a man's worldly success will be in the measure that he sacrifices his confused animal thoughts, and fixes his mind on the development of his plans, and the strengthening of his resolution and self-reliance. And the higher he lifts his thoughts, the more manly, upright, and righteous he becomes, the greater will be his success, the more blessed and enduring will be his achievements.

The universe does not favor the greedy, the dishonest, the vicious, although on the mere surface it may sometimes appear to do so; it helps the honest, the magnanimous, the virtuous. All the great Teachers of the ages have declared this in varying forms, and to prove and know it a man has but to persist in making himself more and more virtuous by lifting up his thoughts.

Intellectual achievements are the result of thought consecrated to the search for knowledge, or for the beautiful and true in life and nature. Such achievements may be sometimes connected with vanity and ambition, but they are not the outcome of those characteristics; they are the natural outgrowth of long and arduous effort, and of pure and unselfish thoughts.

Spiritual achievements are the consummation of holy aspirations. He who lives constantly in the conception of noble and lofty thoughts, who dwells upon all that is pure and unselfish, will, as surely as the sun reaches its zenith and the moon its full, become wise and noble in character, and rise into a position of influence and blessedness.

Achievement, of whatever kind, is the crown of effort, the diadem of thought. By the aid of self-control, resolution, purity, righteousness, and well-directed thought a man ascends; by the aid of animality, indolence, impurity, corruption, and confusion of thought a man descends.

A man may rise to high success in the world, and even to lofty altitudes in the spiritual realm, and again descend into weakness and wretchedness by allowing arrogant, selfish, and corrupt thoughts to take possession of him.

Victories attained by right thought can only be maintained by watchfulness. Many give way when success is assured, and rapidly fall back into failure.

All achievements, whether in the business, intellectual, or spiritual world, are the result of definitely directed thought, are governed by the same law and are of the same method; the only difference lies in *the object of attainment*.

He who would accomplish little must sacrifice little; he who would achieve much must sacrifice much; he who would attain highly must sacrifice greatly.

Visions and Ideals

The dreamers are the saviors of the world. As the visible world is sustained by the invisible, so men, through all their trials and sins and sordid vocations, are nourished by the beautiful visions of their solitary dreamers. Humanity cannot forget its dreamers; it cannot let their ideals fade and die; it lives in them; it knows them as the *realities* which it shall one day see and know.

Composer, sculptor, painter, poet, prophet, sage, these are the makers of the afterworld, the architects of heaven. The world is beautiful because they have lived; without them, laboring humanity would perish.

He who cherishes a beautiful vision, a lofty ideal in his heart, will one day realize it. Columbus cherished a vision of another world, and he discovered it; Copernicus fostered the vision of a multiplicity of worlds and a wider universe, and he revealed it; Buddha beheld the vision of a spiritual world of stainless beauty and perfect peace, and he entered into it.

Cherish your visions; cherish your ideals; cherish the music that stirs in your heart, the beauty that forms in your mind, the loveliness that drapes your purest thoughts, for out of them will grow all delightful conditions, all heavenly environment; of these, if you but remain true to them, your world will at last be built.

To desire is to obtain; to aspire is to achieve. Shall man's basest desires receive the fullest measure of gratification, and his purest aspirations starve for lack of sustenance? Such is not the Law: such a condition of things can never obtain: "Ask and receive."

Dream lofty dreams, and as you dream, so shall you become. Your Vision is the promise of what you shall one day be; your Ideal is the prophecy of what you shall at last unveil.

The greatest achievement was at first and for a time a dream. The oak sleeps in the acorn; the bird waits in the egg; and in the highest vision of the soul a waking angel stirs. Dreams are the seedlings of realities.

Your circumstances may be uncongenial, but they shall not long remain so if you but perceive an Ideal and strive to reach it. You cannot travel *within* and stand still *without*. Here is a youth hard pressed by poverty and labor; Confined long hours in an unhealthy workshop; unschooled, and lacking all the arts of refinement. But he dreams of better things: he thinks of intelligence, of refinement, of grace and beauty. He conceives of, mentally builds up, an ideal condition of life; the vision of a wider liberty and a larger scope takes possession of him; unrest urges him to action, and he utilizes all his spare time and means, small though they are, to the development of his latent powers and resources. Very soon so altered has his mind become that the workshop can no longer hold him. It has become so out of harmony with his mentality that it falls out of his life as a garment is cast aside, and, with the growth of opportunities which fit the scope of his expanding powers, he passes out of it forever. Years later we see this youth as a full-grown man. We find him a master of certain forces of the mind which he wields with worldwide influence and almost unequaled power. In his hands he holds the cords of gigantic responsibilities; he speaks, and lo! lives are changed; men and women hang upon his words and remold their characters, and, sunlike, he becomes the fixed and luminous center around which innumerable destinies revolve. He has realized the Vision of his youth. He has become one with his Ideal.

And you, too, youthful reader, will realize the Vision (not the idle wish) of your heart, be it base or beautiful, or a mixture of both, for you will always gravitate toward that which you, secretly, most love. Into your hands will be placed the exact results of your own thoughts; you will receive that which you earn; no more, no less. Whatever your present environment may be, you will fall, remain, or rise with your thoughts, your Vision, your Ideal. You will become as small as your controlling desire; as great as your dominant aspiration: in the beautiful words of Stanton Kirkham Davis, "You may be keeping accounts, and presently you shall walk out of the door that for so long has seemed to you the barrier of your ideals, and shall find yourself before an audience—the pen still behind your ear, the ink stains on your fingers—and then and there shall pour out the torrent of your inspiration. You may be driving sheep, and you shall wander to the city—bucolic and open mouthed; shall wander under the intrepid guidance of the spirit into the studio of the master, and after a time he shall say, 'I have nothing more to teach you.' And now you have become the master, who did so recently dream of great things while driving sheep. You shall lay down the saw and the plane to take upon yourself the regeneration of the world."

The thoughtless, the ignorant, and the indolent, seeing only the apparent effects of things and not the things themselves, talk of luck, of fortune, and chance. Seeing a man grow rich, they say, "How lucky he is!" Observing another become intellectual, they exclaim, "How highly favored he is!" And noting the saintly character and wide influence of another, they remark, "How chance aids him at every turn!" They do not see the trials and failures and struggles which these men have voluntarily encountered in order to gain their experience; have no knowledge of the sacrifices they have made, of the undaunted efforts they have put forth, of the faith they have exercised, that they might overcome the apparently insurmountable, and realize the Vision of their heart. They do not know the darkness and the heartaches; they only see the light and joy, and call it "luck"; do not see the long and arduous journey, but only behold the pleasant goal, and call it "good fortune"; do not understand the process, but only perceive the result, and call it "chance."

In all human affairs there are *efforts*, and there are *results*, and the strength of the effort is the measure of the result. Chance is not. "Gifts," powers, material, intellectual, and spiritual possessions are the fruits of effort; they are thoughts completed, objects accomplished, visions realized.

The Vision that you glorify in your mind, the Ideal that you enthrone in your heart—this you will build your life by, this you will become.

Serenity

Calmness of mind is one of the beautiful jewels of wisdom. It is the result of long and patient effort in self-control. Its presence is an indication of ripened experience, and of a more than ordinary knowledge of the laws and operations of thought.

A man becomes calm in the measure that he understands himself as a thought-evolved being, for such knowledge necessitates the understanding of others as the result of thought, and as he develops a right understanding, and sees more and more clearly the internal relations of things by the action of cause and effect, he ceases to fuss and fume and worry and grieve, and remains poised, steadfast, serene.

The calm man, having learned how to govern himself, knows how to adapt himself to others; and they, in turn, reverence his spiritual strength, and feel that they can learn of him and rely upon him. The more tranquil a man becomes, the greater is his success, his influence, his power for good. Even the ordinary trader will find his business prosperity increase as he develops a greater self-control and equanimity, for people will always prefer to deal with a man whose demeanor is strongly equable.

The strong, calm man is always loved and revered. He is like a shade-giving tree in a thirsty land, or a sheltering rock in a storm. "Who does not love a tranquil heart, a sweet-tempered, balanced life? It does not matter whether it rains or shines, or what changes come to those possessing these blessings, for they are always sweet, serene, and calm. That exquisite poise of character which we call serenity is the last lesson of culture; it is the flowering of life, the fruitage of the soul. It is precious as wisdom, more to be desired than gold—yea, than even fine gold. How insignificant mere money-seeking looks in comparison with a serene life—a life that dwells in the ocean of Truth, beneath the waves, beyond the reach of tempests, in the Eternal Calm!

"How many people we know who sour their lives, who ruin all that is sweet and beautiful by explosive tempers, who destroy their poise of character, and make bad blood! It is a question whether the great majority of people do not ruin their lives and mar their happiness by lack of self-control. How few people we meet in life who are well-balanced, who have that exquisite poise which is characteristic of the finished character!"

Yes, humanity surges with uncontrolled passion, is tumultuous with ungoverned grief, is blown about by anxiety and doubt. Only the wise man, only he whose thoughts are controlled and purified, makes the winds and the storms of the soul obey him.

Tempest-tossed souls, wherever ye may be, under whatsoever conditions ye may live, know this—in the ocean of life the isles of Blessedness are smiling, and the sunny shore of your ideal awaits your coming. Keep your hand firmly upon the helm of thought. In the bark of your soul reclines the commanding Master; He does but sleep; wake Him. Self-control is strength; Right Thought is mastery; Calmness is power. Say unto your heart, "Peace, be still!"

V

"Right Beginnings"

◆→✦→◆

(from *Byways of Blessedness*, 1904)

Allen was a moral and practical philosopher as a well as a mystic. In this essay he celebrates the power of beginning a task with the right kind of precision and dedication: "Successful men, influential men, good men are those who, among other things, have learned the value and utilized the power hidden in the obscure beginnings that the foolish man passes by as insignificant." I once interviewed legendary basketball coach John Wooden (1910–2010), who led UCLA to a string of unprecedented victories. Wooden would open the first day's practice of each season by teaching his hotshot recruits the proper way to put their socks on. By rolling your socks up the right way you avoid blisters and are nimbler on your feet. Wooden recognized that the way you approach beginnings is the way you approach the whole. He could have been echoing James Allen.

—MH

Right Beginnings

All common things, each day's events,
That with the hour begin and end;
Our pleasures and our discontents
Are rounds by which we may ascend.
We have not wings, we cannot soar;
But we have feet to scale and climb.

—Longfellow

For common life its wants
And ways, would I set forth in beauteous hues.

—Browning

Life is full of beginnings. They are presented every day and every hour to every person. Most beginnings are small and appear trivial and insignificant, but in reality they are the most important things in life.

See how in the material world everything proceeds from small beginnings. The mightiest river is at first a rivulet over which the grasshopper could leap; the great flood commences with a few drops of rain; the sturdy oak, that has endured the storms of a thousand winters, was once an acorn.

Consider how in the spiritual world the greatest things proceed from smallest beginnings. A light fancy may be the inception of a wonderful invention or an immortal work of art; a spoken sentence may turn the tide of history; a pure thought entertained may lead to the exercise of a world-wide regenerative power.

Have you yet discovered the vast importance of beginnings? Do you really know what is involved in a beginning? Do you know the number of beginnings you are continuously making, and do you realize their full import? If not, come with me for a short time, thoughtfully to explore this much ignored byway of blessedness; for blessed it is when wisely resorted to, and much strength and comfort it holds for the understanding mind.

A beginning is a cause, and as such it must be followed by an effect or a train of effects, and the effect will be of the same nature as the cause. The nature of an initial impulse determines the body of its results. A beginning also presupposes an ending, a consummation, achievement, or goal. A gate leads to a path, and the path to some particular destination; so a beginning leads to results, and results lead to a completion.

There are right beginnings and wrong beginnings, followed by effects of a like nature. You can, by careful thought, avoid wrong beginnings and make right beginnings, and so escape evil results and enjoy good results.

There are beginnings over which you have no control and authority—these are without, in the universe, in the world of nature around you, and in other people possessing the same liberty as yourself.

Do not concern yourself with these beginnings, but direct your energies and attention to those beginnings over which you have complete control and authority, which bring about the complicated web of results which compose your life. These beginnings are to be found in the realm of your own thoughts and actions; in your mental attitude toward the variety of circumstances through which you pass; in your conduct day by day—in short, in your life as you make it, which is your world of good or ill.

In aiming at the life of Blessedness one of the simplest beginnings to be considered and rightly made is that which we all make every day—the beginning of each day's life.

How do you begin each day? At what hour do you rise? How do you begin your work? In what frame of mind do you enter upon the sacred life of a new day? What answer can you give your heart to these important questions? You will find that much happiness or unhappiness follows upon the right or wrong beginning of the day, and that, when every day is wisely begun, happy and harmonious sequences will mark its course, and life in its totality will not fall far short of the ideal blessedness.

It is a right and strong beginning of the day to rise at an early hour. Even if your worldly work does not demand it, it is wise to make of it a habit, and begin the day strongly by shaking off indolence and by putting on vigor and energy. How are you to develop strength of will and mind and body if you begin every day by yielding to weakness? Self-indulgence is followed by unhappiness.

Those who lie a-bed till late are not necessarily bright and cheerful and fresh, but often the prey of irritabilities, depressions, debilities, nervous disorders, abnormal fancies, and all unhappy moods.

This is the heavy price they have to pay for their daily indulgence. Yet, so blinding is the pandering to self that, like the man taking his daily dram in the belief that it is bracing the nerves which it is all the time shattering, so the lie-a-bed is convinced that long hours of ease are necessary for him as a possible remedy for those very moods and weaknesses and disorders of which his indulgence is the cause. Men and women are unaware of the losses that they entail upon themselves by this common indulgence: loss of strength both of mind and body, loss of prosperity, loss of knowledge, and loss of happiness.

Begin the day by rising early. If you have no object in doing so, never mind; arise, go for a gentle walk among the beauties of nature, and you will experience a buoyancy, a freshness, and a delight, not to say a peace of mind, that will reward you for your effort. One good effort is followed by another; and when a man begins the day by rising early, even though with no other purpose in view, he will find the silent early hour so conducive to clearness of mind and calmness of thought, his early morning walk so profitable in enabling

him to become a consecutive thinker and so to see life and
its problems, as well as himself and his affairs, in a clearer
light; that in time he will rise early for the express purpose of
preparing and harmonizing his mind to meet any and every
difficulty with wisdom and calm strength.

There is, indeed, so spiritual an influence in the early
morning hour, so divine a silence and inexpressible repose,
that he who, purposeful and strong, throws off the mantle
of ease and climbs the hills to greet the morning sun will
thereby climb no inconsiderable distance up the hills of blessedness and truth.

The right beginning of the day will be followed by cheerfulness at the first meal, permeating the household with a
sunny influence; and the work of the day will be undertaken
in a strong and confident spirit, and the whole day will be
well lived.

There is also a sense in which every day is to be regarded
as the beginning of a new life, in which one can think, act,
and live newly, and in a wiser and better spirit.

Every day is a fresh beginning;
Every morn is the world made new.
Ye who are weary of sorrow and sinning,
Here is a beautiful hope for you,
A hope for me and a hope for you.

Do not dwell upon the sins and mistakes of yesterday
so exclusively as to have no energy and mind left for living
rightly today, and do not think that the sins of yesterday can

prevent you from living aright today. Begin today right with the world, and aided by the accumulated experiences of all your past days, live it better than any of your previous days; but you cannot possibly live it better unless you begin it better. The character of the whole day depends upon the way it is begun.

Another beginning of great importance is the beginning of any particular and responsible undertaking. How does a man begin the building of a house? He secures a plan of the proposed edifice, and proceeds to build according to the plan, scrupulously following it in every detail, from the foundation up. Should he neglect the beginning—the obtaining of an architectural plan—his labor would be wasted, and his building, should it reach completion without tumbling to pieces, would be insecure and worthless. The same law holds good in any important work: the right beginning and first essential is a definite mental plan on which to build. Nature will have no slip-shod work, no slovenliness, and she annihilates confusion, or rather, confusion is in itself annihilation. Order, definiteness, purpose, eternally and universally prevail; and he who in his operations ignores these elements of precision at once deprives himself of substantiality, completeness, success.

> *Life without a plan,*
> *As useless as the moment it began,*
> *Serves merely as a soil for discontent*
> *To thrive in, an encumbrance ere half spent.*

Let a man start in business without having in his mind a well formed plan to pursue systematically, and he will be incoherent in his efforts and must fail in his business operations. The laws to be observed in the building of a house also operate in the building up of a business. A definite plan is followed by coherent effort; and coherent effort is followed by well-knit and orderly results—completeness, perfection, success, happiness.

But not only mechanical and commercial enterprise—all undertakings, of whatsoever nature, come under this law. The author's book, the artist's picture, the orator's speech, the reformer's work, the inventor's machine, the general's campaign, are all carefully organized and planned in the mind before the attempt to actualize them is commenced; and in accordance with the unity, solidarity, and perfection of the original mental plan will be the actual and ultimate success of the undertaking.

Successful men, influential men, good men are those who, among other things, have learned the value and utilized the power hidden in the obscure beginnings that the foolish man passes by as insignificant.

But the most important beginning of all—that upon which affliction or blessedness inevitably depends, yet the one most neglected and least understood—is the inception of thought in the hidden, but causal, region of the mind. Your whole life is a series of effects, having their cause in thought—in your own thought. All conduct is made and moulded by thought; all deeds, good or bad, are thoughts made visible. A seed put into the ground is the beginning of a plant or tree; the seed germinates, the plant or tree comes forth into the light and evolves. A thought put into the mind is the beginning of a line of conduct: the thought first sends down its roots into the mind, thence to push forth into the light in the form of actions or conduct, which evolve into character and destiny.

Loving, gentle, kind, unselfish, and pure thoughts are right beginnings, leading to blissful results.

This is so simple, so plain, so absolutely true; and yet how neglected, how evaded, and how little understood!

The gardener who most carefully studies how, when, and where to put in his seeds gains the greater horticultural knowledge and obtains the best results. The best crops gladden the soul of him who makes the best beginning. The man who most patiently studies how to put into his mind the seeds of strong, wholesome, and charitable thoughts, will obtain the best results in life, and gain the greater knowledge of truth. The greatest blessedness comes to him who infuses into his mind the purest and noblest thoughts.

None but right acts can follow right thoughts; none but a right life can follow right acts—and by living a right life all blessedness is achieved.

He who considers the nature and import of his thoughts, who strives daily to eliminate bad thoughts and supplant them with good, comes at last to see that thoughts are the beginnings of results which affect every fibre of his being, which potently influence every event and circumstance of his life. And when he thus sees, he thinks only right thoughts, chooses to make only those mental beginnings which lead to peace and blessedness.

Wrong thoughts are painful in their inception, painful in their growth, and painful in their fruitage. Right thoughts are blissful in their inception, blissful in their growth, and blissful in their fruitage.

Many are the right beginnings which a man must discover and adopt on his way to wisdom; but that which is first and last, most important and all-embracing, which is the source and fountain of all abiding happiness, is the right beginning of the mental operations—this implies the steady development of self-control, willpower, steadfastness, strength, purity, gentleness, insight, and comprehension. It leads to the perfecting of life, for he who thinks perfectly has abolished all unhappiness, his every moment is peaceful, his years are rounded with bliss—he has attained to the complete and perfect blessedness.

VI
"Small Tasks and Duties"

———✦◈✦◈✦———

(from *Byways of Blessedness*, 1904)

A friend once told me, "The way you do one thing is the way you do everything." The moment I heard that I made it into a personal motto. In thirty years I have not seen it once proven wrong. I have literally never witnessed someone who excelled at small tasks and checking of details who did not also excel at large tasks. Negligence of detail is likewise consistent throughout all tasks. If you want to be great, you must do small things in a great way. That is the essential point of Allen's essay. Although he quotes Confucius to support this principle, he could just as easily have quoted the Hermetic dictum, "As above, so below." That is a universal truth for all spheres of existence. This chapter features what I consider one of Allen's finest insights: "You do not live your life in the mass; you live it in the fragments, and from these the mass emerges."

—MH

Small Tasks and Duties

Wrapped in our nearest duty is the key
Which shall unlock for us the Heavenly Gate:
Unveiled, the Heavenly Vision he shall see.
Who cometh not too early or too late.

Like the star
That shines afar,
Without haste
And without rest,
Let each man wheel with steady sway
Round the task that rules the day,
And do his best.

—Goethe

As pain and bliss inevitably follow on wrong and right beginnings, so unhappiness and blessedness are inseparably bound up with small tasks and duties. Not that a duty has any power of itself to bestow happiness or the reverse—this is contained in the attitude of mind which is assumed toward the duty—and everything depends upon the way in which it is approached and done.

Not only great happiness but great power arises from doing little things unselfishly, wisely, and perfectly, for life in its totality is made up of little things. Wisdom inheres in the common details of everyday existence, and when the parts are made perfect the Whole will be without blemish.

Everything in the universe is made up of little things, and the perfection of the great is based upon the perfection of the small. If any detail of the universe were imperfect the Whole would be imperfect. If any particle were omitted the aggregate would cease to be. Without a grain of dust there could be no world, and the world is perfect because the grain of dust is perfect. Neglect of the small is confusion of the great. The snowflake is as perfect as the star; the dewdrop is as symmetrical as the planet; the microbe is not less mathematically proportioned than the man. By laying stone upon stone, plumbing and fitting each with perfect adjustment, the temple at last stands forth in all its architectural beauty. The small precedes the great. The small is not merely the apologetic attendant of the great, it is its master and informing genius.

Vain men are ambitious to be great, and look about to do some great thing, ignoring and despising the little tasks which call for immediate attention, and in the doing of which there is no vainglory, regarding such "trivialities" as beneath the notice of great men. The fool lacks knowledge because he lacks humility, and, inflated with the thought of self-importance, he aims at impossible things.

The great man has become such by the scrupulous and unselfish attention which he has given to small duties. He has become wise and powerful by sacrificing ambition and pride in the doing of those necessary things which evoke no applause and promise no reward. He never sought greatness; he sought faithfulness, unselfishness, integrity, truth; and in finding these in the common round of small tasks and duties he unconsciously ascended to the level of greatness.

The great man knows the vast value that inheres in moments, words, greetings, meals, apparel, correspondence, rest, work, detached efforts, fleeting obligations, in the thousand-and-one little things which press upon him for attention—briefly, in the common details of life. He sees everything as divinely apportioned, needing only the application of dispassionate thought and action on his part to render life blessed and perfect. He neglects nothing, does not hurry; seeks to escape nothing but error and folly; attends to every duty as it is presented to him, and does not postpone and regret. By giving himself unreservedly to his nearest duty, forgetting alike pleasure and pain, he attains to that combined childlike simplicity and unconscious power which is greatness.

The advice of Confucius to his disciples: "Eat at your own table as you would at the table of a king," emphasises the immeasurable importance of little things, as also does that aphorism of another great teacher, Buddha: "If anything is to be done, let a man do it, let him attack it vigorously."

To neglect small tasks, or to execute them in a perfunctory or slovenly manner, is a mark of weakness and folly.

The giving of one's entire and unselfish attention to every duty in its proper place evolves, by a natural growth, higher and ever higher combinations of duties, because it evolves power and develops talent, genius, goodness, character. A man ascends into greatness as naturally and unconsciously as the plant evolves a flower, and in the same manner, by fitting with unabated energy and diligence, every effort and detail in its proper place, thus harmonizing his life and character without friction or waste of power.

Of the almost innumerable recipes for the development of "will-power" and "concentration" which are now scattered abroad, one looks almost in vain for any wholesome hint applicable to vital experience. "Breathings," "postures," "visualisings," "occult methods" are practices as delusive as they are artificial and remote from all that is real and essential in life; while the true path of—path of duty, of earnest and undivided application to one's daily task—along which alone will-power and concentration of thought can be wholesomely and normally developed, remains unknown, untrodden, unexplored even by the elect.

All unnatural forcing and straining in order to gain "power" should be abandoned. There is no way from childhood to manhood but by growth; nor is there any other way from folly to wisdom, from ignorance to knowledge, from weakness to strength. A man must learn how to grow little by little and day after day, by adding thought to thought, effort to effort, deed to deed.

It is true the fakir gains some sort of power by his long persistence in "postures," and "mortifications," but it is a power which is bought at a heavy price, and that price is an equal loss of strength in another direction. He is never a strong, useful character, but a mere fantastic specialist in some psychological trick. He is not a developed man, he is a maimed man.

True will-power consists in overcoming the irritabilities, follies, rash impulses, and moral lapses which accompany the daily life of the individual, and which are apt to manifest themselves on every slight provocation; and in developing calmness, self-possession, and dispassionate action in the press and heat of worldly duties, and in the midst of the passionate and unbalanced throng.

Anything short of this is not true power, and this can only be developed along the normal pathway of steady growth in executing ever more and more masterfully, unselfishly, and perfectly the daily round of legitimate tasks and pressing obligations.

The master is not he whose "psychological accomplishments," rounded by mystery and wonder, leave him in unguarded moments the prey of irritability, of regret, of peevishness, or other petty folly or vice, but he whose "mastery" is manifested in fortitude, non-resentment, steadfastness, calmness, and Infinite patience. The true Master is master of himself; anything other than this is not mastery but delusion.

The man who sets his whole mind on the doing of each task as it is presented, who puts into it energy and intelligence, shutting all else out from his mind, and striving to do that one thing, no matter how small, completely and perfectly, detaching himself from all reward in his task—that man will every day be acquiring greater command over his mind, and will, by ever-ascending degrees, become at last a man of power—a Master.

Put yourself unreservedly into your present task, and so work, so act, so live that you shall leave each task a finished piece of labor—this is the true way to the acquisition of will-power, concentration of thought, and conservation of energy. Look not about for magical formulas, for strained and artificial methods. Every resource is already with you and within you. You have but to learn how wisely to apply yourself in that place which you now occupy. Until this is done those other and higher places which are waiting for you cannot be taken possession of, cannot be reached.

There is no way to strength and wisdom but by acting strongly and wisely in the present moment, and each present moment reveals its own task. The great man, the wise man, does small things greatly, regarding nothing as "trivial" that is necessary. The weak man, the foolish man, does small things carelessly and meanly, hankering the while after some greater work for which, in his neglect and inability in small matters, he is ceaselessly advertising his incapacity. The man who least governs himself is always more ambitious to govern others and assume important responsibilities.

"Whoso neglects a thing which he suspects he ought to do because it seems too small a thing is deceiving himself; it is not too little but too great for him that he doeth it not."

And just as the strong doing of small tasks leads to greater strength, so the doing of those tasks weakly leads to greater weakness. What a man is in his fractional duties that he is in the aggregate of his character. Weakness is as great a source of suffering as sin, and there can be no true blessedness until some measure of strength of character is evolved. The weak man becomes strong by attaching value to little things and doing them accordingly. The strong man becomes weak by falling into looseness and neglect concerning small things, thereby forfeiting his simple wisdom and squandering his energy. Herein we see the beneficent operation of that law of growth which is expressed in the little-understood words: "To him that hath shall be given, and from him that hath not shall be taken away even that which he hath." Man instantly gains or loses by every thought he thinks, every word he says, every act he does, and every work to which he puts hand and heart.

His character from moment to moment is a graduating quantity, to or from which some measure of good is added or subtracted during every moment, and the gain or loss is involved, even to absoluteness, in each thought, word, and deed as these follow each other in rapid sequence.

He who masters the small becomes the rightful possessor of the great. He who is mastered by the small can achieve no superlative victory.

Life is a kind of co-operative trust in which the whole is of the nature of, and dependent upon, the unit.

A successful business, a perfect machine, a glorious temple, or a beautiful character is evolved from the perfect adjustment of a multiplicity of parts.

The foolish man thinks that little faults, little indulgences, little sins, are of no consequence; he persuades himself that so long as he does not commit flagrant immoralities he is virtuous, and even holy; but he is thereby deprived of virtue and holiness, and the world knows him accordingly; it does not reverence, adore, and love him; it passes him by; he is reckoned of no account; his influence is destroyed. The efforts of such a man to make the world virtuous, his exhortations to his fellow-men to abandon great vices, are empty of substance and barren of fruitage. The insignificance which he attaches to his small vices permeates his whole character and is the measure of his manhood: he is regarded as an insignificant man. The levity with which he commits his errors and publishes his weakness comes back to him in the form of neglect and loss of influence and respect: he is not sought after, for who will seek to be taught of folly? His work does not prosper, for who will lean upon a reed? His words fall upon deaf ears, for they are void of practice, wisdom, and experience, and who will go after an echo?

The wise man, or he who is becoming wise, sees the danger which lurks in those common personal faults which men mostly commit thoughtlessly and with impunity; he also sees the salvation which inheres in the abandonment of those faults, as well as in the practice of virtuous thoughts and acts which the majority disregard as unimportant, and in those quiet but momentous daily conquests over self which are hidden from other's eyes.

He who regards his smallest delinquencies as of the gravest nature becomes a saint. He sees the far-reaching influence, good or bad, which extends from his every thought and act, and how he himself is made or unmade by the soundness or unsoundness of those innumerable details of conduct which combine to form his character and life, and so he watches, guards, purifies, and perfects himself little by little and step by step.

As the ocean is composed of drops, the earth of grains, and the stars of points of light, so is life composed of thoughts and acts; without these life would not be. Every man's life, therefore, is what his apparently detached thoughts and acts make it. Their combination is himself. As the year consists of a given number of sequential moments, so a man's character and life consists of a given number of sequential thoughts and deeds, and the finished whole will bear the impress of the parts.

All sorts of things and weather
Must be taken in together,
To make up a year
And a sphere.

Little kindnesses, generosities, and sacrifices make up a kind and generous character. Little renunciations, endurances and victories over self make up a strong and noble character. The truly honest man is honest in the minutest details of his life. The noble man is noble in every little thing he says and does.

It is a fatal delusion with men to think that life is detached from the momentary thought and act, and not to understand that the passing thought and deed is the foundation and substance of life. When this is fully understood all things are seen as sacred, and every act becomes religious. Truth is wrapped up in Infinitesimal details. Thoroughness is genius.

> *Possessions vanish, and opinions change,*
> *And passions hold a fluctuating seat:*
> *But, by the storms or circumstance unshaken,*
> *And subject neither to eclipse nor wane,*
> *Duty exists.*

You do not live your life in the mass; you live it in the fragments, and from these the mass emerges. You can will to live each fragment nobly if you choose, and, this being done, there can be no particle of baseness in the finished whole. The saying "Take care of the pence and the pounds will take care of themselves" is seen to be more than worldly-wise when applied spiritually, for, to take care of the present, passing act, knowing that by so doing the total sum and amount of life and character will be safely preserved, is to be divinely wise. Do not long to do great and laudable things; these will do themselves if you do your present task nobly. Do not chafe at the restrictions and limitations of your present duty, but be nobly unselfish in the doing of it, putting aside discontent, listlessness, and the foolish contemplation of great deeds which lie beyond you—and lo! already the greatness for which you sighed begins to appear. There is no weakness like peevishness. Aspire to the attainment of inward nobility, not outward glory, and begin to attain it where you now are.

The irksomeness and sting which you feel to be in your task are in your mind only. Alter your attitude of mind toward it, and at once the crooked path is made straight, the unhappiness is turned into joy.

See that your every fleeting moment is strong, pure, and purposeful; put earnestness and unselfishness into every passing task and duty; make your every thought, word, and deed sweet and true; thus learning, by practice and experience, the inestimable value of the small things of life, you will gather, little by little, abundant and enduring blessedness.

VII
Out from the Heart

✦❖✦

(complete text, 1904)

I encourage every reader of As a Man Thinketh *to read this short work in tandem with its more famous predecessor.* Out from the Heart *expands upon the thesis that* you are as your mind is. *The essay contains a stirring message of self-governance and also one of my favorite passages from Allen's work:*

> *Mind is the arbiter of life; it is the creator and shaper of conditions, and the recipient of its own results. It contains within itself both the power to create illusion and to perceive reality.*
>
> *Mind is the infallible weaver of destiny; thought is the thread, good and evil deeds are the warp and woof, and the web, woven upon the*

loom of life, is character. Mind clothes itself in garments of its own making.

This essay marries New Thought mysticism with the Victorian ethics of self-sufficiency and moral education. Those principles were part of Allen's outlook, too. That said, Allen was a social reformer who believed in laws protecting workers and promoting social equity. He was the complete man for his age. And ours.

—MH

Foreword

Confucius said, "The perfecting of one's self is the fundamental base of all progress and all moral development;" a maxim as profound and comprehensive as it is simple, practical, and uninvolved, for there is no surer way to knowledge, nor no better way to help the world than by perfecting one's self. Nor is there any nobler work or higher science than that of self-perfection. He who studies how to become faultless, who strives to be pure-hearted, who aims at the possession of a calm, wise, and seeing mind, engages in the most sublime task that man can undertake, and the results of which are perceptible in a well-ordered, blessed, and beautiful life.

—James Allen

The Heart
and the Life

As the heart, so is the life. The within is ceaselessly becoming the without. Nothing remains unrevealed. That which is hidden is but for a time; it ripens and comes forth at last. Seed, tree, blossom, and fruit is the fourfold order of the universe. From the state of a man's heart proceed the conditions of his life; his thoughts blossom into deeds, and his deeds bear the fruitage of character and destiny.

Life is ever unfolding from within, and revealing itself to the light, and thoughts engendered in the heart at last reveal themselves in words, actions, and things accomplished.

As the fountain from the hidden spring, so issues man's life from the secret recesses of his heart. All that he is and does is generated there. All that he will be and do will take its rise there.

Sorrow and gladness, suffering and enjoyment, hope and fear, hatred and love, ignorance and enlightenment, are nowhere but in the heart; they are solely mental conditions.

Man is the keeper of his heart; the watcher of his mind; the solitary sentinel of his citadel of life. As such, he can be diligent or negligent. He can keep his heart more and more carefully; he can more strenuously watch and purify his mind; and he can guard himself against the thinking of unrighteous thoughts: this is the way of enlightenment and bliss. On the other hand, he can live loosely and carelessly, neglecting the supreme task of rightly ordering his life: this is the way of self-delusion and suffering.

Let a man realize that life in its totality proceeds from the mind, and lo, the way of blessedness is opened up to him! For he will then discover that he possesses the power to rule his mind, and to fashion it in accordance with his Ideal. So will be elect to strongly and steadfastly walk those pathways of thought and action which are altogether excellent; to him life will become beautiful and sacred; and, sooner or later, he will put to flight all evil, confusion and suffering; for it is impossible for a man to fall short of liberation, enlightenment, and peace, who guards with unwearying diligence the gateway of his heart.

The Nature and Power of Mind

Mind is the arbiter of life; it is the creator and shaper of conditions, and the recipient of its own results. It contains within itself both the power to create illusion and to perceive reality.

Mind is the infallible weaver of destiny; thought is the thread, good and evil deeds are the warp and woof, and the web, woven upon the loom of life, is character. Mind clothes itself in garments of its own making.

Man, as a mental being, possesses all the powers of mind, and is furnished with illimitable choice. He learns by experience, and he can accelerate or retard his experience. He is not arbitrarily bound at any point, but he has bound himself at many points, and having bound himself he can, when he chooses, liberate himself. He can become bestial or pure, ignoble or noble, foolish or wise, just as he chooses. He can, by recurring practice, form habits, and he can, by renewed effort, break them off. He can surround himself with illusions until Truth is completely lost, and he can destroy one and another of those illusions until Truth is entirely recovered. His possibilities are limitless; his freedom is complete.

It is in the nature of mind to create its own conditions, and to choose the states in which it shall dwell. It also has the power to alter any condition and to abandon any state, and this it is continually doing as it gathers knowledge of state after state by repeated choice and exhaustive experience.

Inward processes of thought make up the sum of character and life, and man can modify and alter these processes by bringing will and effort to bear upon them. The bonds of habit, impotence, and sin are self-made, and can only be destroyed by one's self; they exist nowhere but in one's mind, and although they are directly related to outward things, they have no real existence in those things. The outer is moulded and vivified by the inner, and never the inner by the outer. Temptation does not arise in the outer object, but in the lust of the mind for that object; nor do suffering and sorrow inhere in the external things and happenings of life, but in an undisciplined attitude of mind toward those things and happenings. The mind that is disciplined by Purity and fortified by Wisdom, avoids all those lusts and desires which are inseparably bound up with affliction, and so arrives at enlightenment and peace.

To condemn others as evil, and to rail against outside conditions as the source of evil, increases, and does not lessen, the world's suffering and unrest. The outer is but the shadow and effect of the inner, and when the heart is pure all outward things are pure.

All growth and life is from within outward; all decay and death is from without inward; this is a universal law. All evolution proceeds from within. All adjustment must take place within. He who ceases to strive against others, and employs his powers in the transformation, regeneration, and development of his own mind, conserves his energies and preserves himself; and as he succeeds in harmonizing his own mind, he leads others by consideration and charity into a like blessed state, for not by assuming authority and guidance over other minds is the way of enlightenment and peace discovered, but by exercising a lawful authority over one's own, and by guiding one's self in pathways of steadfast and lofty virtue.

A man's life proceeds from his heart, his mind: he has compounded that mind by his own thoughts and deeds: it is in his power to re-fashion that mind by his choice of thought: he can therefore transform his life. Let us see how this is to be done.

Formation of Habit

Every established mental condition is an acquired habit, and it has become such by continuous repetition of thought. Despondency and cheerfulness, anger and calmness, covetousness and generosity—indeed, all states of mind—are habits built up by choice, until they have become automatic. A thought constantly repeated at last becomes a fixed habit of the mind, and from such habits proceeds the life.

It is in the nature of the mind to acquire knowledge by the repetition of its experiences. A thought which it is very difficult, at first, to hold and to dwell upon, at last becomes, by constantly being held in the mind, a natural and habitual condition. Just as a boy, when commencing to learn a trade, cannot even handle his tools aright, much less use them correctly, but after long repetition and practice plies them with perfect ease and consummate skill, so a state of mind, at first apparently impossible of realization, is, by perseverance and practice, at last acquired and built into the character as a natural and spontaneous condition.

In this power of the mind to form and re-form its habits, its conditions, is contained the basis of man's salvation, and the open door to perfect liberty by the mastery of self, for as a man has the power to form harmful habits, so he has the same power to create habits that are essentially good. And here we come to a point which needs some elucidating, and which calls for deep and earnest thought on the part of my reader.

It is commonly said to be easier to do wrong than right, to sin than to be holy; such condition has come to be regarded, almost universally, as axiomatic, and no less a teacher than the Buddha has said—"Bad deeds, and deeds hurtful to ourselves, are easy to do; what is beneficial and good, that is very difficult to do,"—and as regards humanity generally, this is true, but it is only true as a passing experience, a fleeting factor in human evolution; it is not a fixed condition of things, is not of the nature of an eternal truth. It is easier for men to do wrong than right, because of the prevalence of ignorance, because the true nature of things, and the essence and meaning of life, are not apprehended. When a child is learning to write, it is extremely easy for it to hold the pen wrongly, and to form its letters incorrectly, but it is painfully difficult to hold the pen and to write properly; and this because of the child's ignorance of the art of writing, which can only be dispelled by persistent effort and practice, until, at last, it becomes natural and easy to hold the pen properly, and to write correctly, and difficult, as well as altogether unnecessary, to do the wrong thing. It is the same in the vital things of mind and life. To think and do rightly requires much practice and renewed effort, but the time at last comes when it becomes habitual and easy to think and do rightly, and difficult, as it is then seen to be altogether unnecessary, to do that which is wrong.

Just as an artisan becomes, by practice, accomplished in his craft, so a man can become, by practice, accomplished in goodness; it is entirely a matter of forming new habits of thought, and he to whom right thoughts have become easy and natural, and wrong thoughts and acts difficult to do, has attained to the highest virtue, to pure, spiritual knowledge.

It is easy and natural for men to sin, because they have formed, by incessant repetition, harmful and unenlightened habits of thought. It is very difficult for the thief to refrain from stealing when opportunity occurs, because he has lived so long in covetous and avaricious thoughts; but such difficulty does not exist for the honest man who has lived so long in upright and honest thoughts, and has thereby become enlightened as to the wrong, folly, and fruitlessness of theft, that even the remotest idea of stealing does not enter his mind. The sin of theft is a very extreme one, and I have introduced it in order to the more clearly illustrate the force and formation of habit; but all sins and virtues are formed in the same way. Anger and impatience are natural and easy to thousands of people, because they are constantly repeating the angry and impatient thought and act, and with each repetition the habit is more firmly established and more deeply rooted. Calmness and patience can become habitual in the same way—by first grasping, through effort, a calm and patient thought, and then continuously thinking it, and living in it, until "use becomes second nature," and anger and impatience pass away for ever. It is thus that every wrong thought may be expelled from the mind; thus that every untrue act may be destroyed; thus that every sin may be overcome.

Doing and Knowing

Let a man realize that his life, in its totality, proceeds from his mind, and that that mind is a combination of habits which he can, by patient effort, modify to any extent, and over which he can thus gain complete ascendancy and control, and he has at once obtained possession of the key which shall open the door to his complete emancipation.

But emancipation from the ills of life (which are the ills of one's mind) is a matter of steady growth from within, and not a sudden acquisition from without. Hourly and daily must the mind be trained to think stainless thoughts, and to adopt right and dispassionate attitudes under those circumstances in which it is prone to fall into wrong and passion. Like the patient sculptor upon his marble, the aspirant to the Right Life must gradually work upon the crude material of his mind until he has wrought out of it the Ideal of his holiest dreams.

In working toward such supreme accomplishment, it is necessary to commence at the lowest and easiest steps, and proceed by natural and progressive stages to the higher and more difficult. This law of growth, progress, evolution, unfoldment, by gradual and ever ascending stages, is absolute in every department of life, and in every human accomplishment, and where it is ignored, total failure will result. In acquiring learning, in learning a trade, or in pursuing a business, this law is fully recognized and minutely obeyed by all; but in acquiring Virtue, in learning Truth, and in pursuing the right conduct and knowledge of life, it is unrecognized and disobeyed by nearly all; hence Virtue, Truth, and the Perfect Life remain unpractised, unacquired, and unknown.

It is a common error to suppose that the Higher Life is a matter of reading, and the adoption of theological or metaphysical hypotheses, and that Spiritual Principles can be apprehended by this method. The Higher Life is a higher living in thought, word, and deed, and the knowledge of those Spiritual Principles, which are imminent in man and in the universe can only be acquired after long discipline in the pursuit and practice of Virtue.

The lesser must be thoroughly grasped and understood before the greater can be known, and practice always precedes real knowledge. The schoolmaster never attempts to teach his pupils the abstract principles of mathematics at the commencement; he knows that by such a method teaching would be vain, and learning impossible. He first places before them a simple sum, and, having explained it, leaves them to do it. When, after repeated failures and ever-renewed effort, they have succeeded in doing it correctly, a more difficult task is set them, and then another and another; and not until the pupils have, through many years of diligent application, mastered all the lessons in arithmetic, does he attempt to unfold to them the underlying mathematical principles.

In learning a trade, say that of a mechanic, the boy is not at first taught the principles of mechanics, but a simple tool is put into his hand and he is told how rightly to use it, and is then left to do it by effort and practice. As he succeeds in plying his tools correctly, more and more difficult tasks are set him, until, after several years of successful practice, he is prepared to study and grasp the principles of mechanics.

In a properly governed household, the child is first taught to be obedient, and to conduct itself properly under all circumstances. The child is not even told why it must do this, but is commanded to do it, and only after it has so far succeeded in doing what is right and proper, is it told why it should do it. No father would attempt to teach his child the principles of ethics before exacting from it the practice of filial duty and social virtue.

Thus practice ever precedes knowledge even in the ordinary things of the world, and in spiritual things, in the living of the Higher Life, this law is rigid in its exactions. Virtue can only be known by doing, and the knowledge of Truth can only be arrived at by perfecting oneself in the practice of Virtue and to be complete in the practice and acquisition of Virtue is to complete in the knowledge of Truth.

Truth can only be arrived at by daily and hourly doing the lessons of Virtue, beginning at the simplest, and passing on to the more difficult; and as a child patiently and obediently learns its lessons at school, constantly practicing, ever exerting itself until all failures and difficulties are surmounted, even so does the child of Truth apply himself to right-doing in thought and action, undaunted by failure, and made stronger by difficulties; and as he succeeds in acquiring Virtue, his mind unfolds itself in the knowledge of Truth, and it is a knowledge in which he can securely rest.

First Steps in
the Higher Life

Seeing that the Path of Virtue is the Path of Knowledge, and that before the all-embracing Principles of Truth can be comprehended, perfection in the more lowly steps must be acquired, how, then, shall a disciple of Truth commence? How shall one who aspires to the righting of his mind and the purification of his heart—that heart which is the fountain and repository of all the issues of life—learn the lessons of Virtue, and thus build himself up in the strength of knowledge, destroying ignorance and the ills of life? What are the first lessons, the first steps? How are they learned? How are they practiced? How are they mastered and understood?

The first lessons consist in overcoming those wrong mental conditions which are most easily eradicated, and which are the common barriers to spiritual progress, as well as in practicing the simple domestic and social virtues; and the reader will be the better aided if I group and classify the first ten steps in three lessons as follows:

VICES TO BE OVERCOME AND ERADICATED.

Vices of the Body

1. Indolence.
2. Self-Indulgence.

First Lesson

Discipline of the Body

Vices of the Tongue

1. Slander.
2. Gossip and idle conversation.
3. Abusive and unkind speech.
4. Levity, or irreverent speech.
5. Captiousness, or fault-finding speech.

Second Lesson

Discipline of Speech

VIRTUES TO BE PRACTICED AND ACQUIRED.

1. Unselfish performance of duty.
2. Unswerving rectitude.
3. Unlimited forgiveness.

Third Lesson

Discipline of Inclination

The two vices of the body, and five of the tongue, are so called because they are manifested in the body and tongue, and also because, by so definitely classifying them, the mind of the reader will be the better helped; but it must be clearly understood that these vices arise primarily in the mind, and are wrong conditions of heart worked out in the body and the tongue.

The existence of such chaotic conditions is an indication that the mind is altogether unenlightened as to the real meaning and purpose of life, and their eradication is the beginning of a virtuous, steadfast, and enlightened life.

But how shall they be overcome and eradicated? By first, and at once, checking and controlling their outward manifestations, by suppressing the wrong act; this will stimulate the mind to watchfulness and reflection until, by repeated practice, it will at last come to perceive and understand the dark and wrong conditions of mind, out of which such acts spring, and will abandon them entirely.

It will be seen that the first step in the discipline of the mind is the overcoming of indolence. This is the easiest step, and until it is perfectly accomplished, the other steps cannot he taken. The clinging to indolence constitutes a complete barrier to the Path of Truth. Indolence consists in giving the body more ease and sleep than it requires, in procrastinating, and in shirking and neglecting those things which should receive immediate attention. This condition of laziness must be overcome by rousing up the body at any early hour, giving it just the amount of sleep it requires for complete recuperation, and by doing promptly and vigorously, every task and duty, no matter how small, as it comes along. On no account should food or drink be taken in bed, and to lie in bed after one has wakened, indulging in ease and reverie, is a habit fatal to promptness and resolution of character, and purity of mind. Nor should one attempt to do his thinking at such a time. Strong, pure, and true thinking is impossible under such circumstances. A man should go to bed to sleep, not to think. He should get up to think and work, not to sleep.

The next step is the overcoming of self-indulgence, or gluttony. The glutton is he who eats for animal gratification only, without considering the true end and object in eating, who eats more than his body requires, and is greedy after sweet things and rich dishes. Such undisciplined desire can only be overcome by reducing the quantity of food eaten, and the number of meals per day, and by resorting to a simple and uninvolved dietary. Regular hours should be set apart for meals, and eating at other times should be rigidly avoided. Suppers should be abolished, as they are altogether unnecessary, and conduce to heavy sleep and cloudiness of mind. The pursuit of such a method of discipline will rapidly bring the hitherto ungoverned appetite under control, and as the sensual sin of self-indulgence is taken out of the mind, the right selection of food will be instinctively and infallibly adapted to the purified mental condition.

It should be well borne in mind that change of heart is the needful thing, and that any change of diet which does not subserve this end is futile. Whilst one eats for enjoyment he is gluttonous. The heart must be purified of sensual craving and gustatory lust.

When the body is well controlled and firmly guided; when that which is to be done is done vigorously; when no task or duty is delayed; when early rising has become a delight; when frugality, temperance, and abstinence are firmly established; when one is contented with the food which is put before him, no matter how scanty and plain, and the craving for gustatory pleasure is at an end—then are the first two steps in the Higher Life accomplished; then is the first great lesson in Truth learned. Thus is established in the heart the foundation of a poised, self-governed, virtuous life.

The next lesson is the lesson of Virtuous Speech, in which are five orderly steps. The first step is the overcoming of slander. Slander consists in inventing or repeating evil reports about others, in exposing and magnifying the faults of others, or of absent friends, and in introducing unworthy insinuations. The elements of thoughtlessness, cruelty, insincerity, and untruthfulness enter into every slanderous act. He who aims at the living of the right life will commence to check the cruel word of slander before it has gone forth from his lips, and will then check and eliminate the insincere thought which gave rise to it. He will watch himself that he does not vilify any, and will refrain from disparaging and condemning the absent friend, whose face he has so recently kissed, or shaken his hand, or smiled into his face. He will not say of another that which he dare not say to him. Thus, coming at last to think sacredly of the character and reputation of others, he will destroy those wrong conditions of mind which give rise to slander.

The next step is the overcoming of gossip and idle conversation. Idle speech consists in talking about the private affairs of others, in talking merely to pass away the time, and in engaging in aimless and irrelevant conversation. Such an ungoverned condition of speech is the outcome of an ill-regulated mind. The man of virtue will bridle his tongue, and thus learn how rightly to govern the mind. He will not let his tongue run idly and foolishly, but will make his speech strong and pure and will either talk with a purpose or remain silent.

Abusive and unkind speech is the next vice to be over-come. The man who abuses and accuses others has himself wandered far from the Right Way. To hurl hard words and names at others is to sink deeply into folly. When a man is inclined to abuse and condemn others, let him restrain his tongue and look in upon himself. The virtuous man refrains from abuse and quarrelling, and employs only words that are useful, necessary, pure, and true.

The next step is the overcoming of levity, or irreverent speech. Light and frivolous talking; the repeating of coarse jokes; the telling of vulgar stories, having no other purpose than to raise an empty laugh; offensive familiarity, and the employment of contemptuous and irreverent terms when speaking to or of others, and particularly of one's elders and those who rank as one's teachers, guardians, or superiors,— all this will be put away by the lover of Virtue and Truth.

Upon the altar of irreverence absent friends and compan-ions are immolated for the passing excitement of a momen-tary laugh, and all the sanctity of life is sacrificed to the zest for ridicule. When respect toward others and the giving of reverence where reverence is due are abandoned, Virtue is abandoned. When modesty, gravity, and dignity are eliminated from speech and behavior, Truth is lost, yea, even its entrance gate is hidden away and forgotten. Irreverence is degrading even in the young, but when it accompanies grey hairs, and appears in the demeanor of the preacher,—this is indeed a piteous spectacle; and when this can be imitated and followed after, then are the blind leading the blind, then have elders and preacher and people lost their way.

The virtuous man will be of grave and reverent speech; he will think and speak of the absent as he thinks and speaks of the dead—tenderly and sacredly; he will put away thoughtlessness, and watch that he does not sacrifice his dignity to gratify a passing impulse to lightness and frivolity. His mirth will be pure and innocent, and his voice will become subdued and musical, and his soul be filled with grace and sweetness as he succeeds in conducting himself as becomes a man of Truth.

The last step in the second lesson is the overcoming of captiousness, or fault-finding speech. This vice of the tongue consists in magnifying and harping on small or apparent faults, in foolish quibbling and hair-splitting, and in pursuing vain arguments based upon groundless suppositions, beliefs, and opinions. Life is short and real, and sin and sorrow and pain are not remedied by carping and contention. The man who is ever on the watch to catch at the words of others in order to contradict and controvert them, has yet to reach the higher way of holiness, the truer life of self-surrender. The man who is ever on the watch to check his own words in order to soften and purify them will find the higher way and the truer life; he will conserve his energies, maintain his composure of mind, and preserve within himself the spirit of Truth.

When the tongue is well controlled and wisely subdued; when selfish impulses and unworthy thoughts no longer rush to the tongue demanding utterance; when the speech has become harmless, pure, gentle, gracious, and purposeful, and no word is uttered but in sincerity and truth,—then are the five steps in virtuous speech accomplished, then is the second great lesson in Truth learned and mastered.

And now some will ask, "But why all this discipline of the body and restraint of the tongue? Surely the Higher Life can be realized and known without such strenuous labor, such incessant effort and watchfulness?" No, it cannot. In the spiritual as the material, nothing is done without labor, and the higher cannot be known until the lower is fulfilled. Can a man make a table before he has learned how to handle a tool and drive a nail? And can a man fashion his mind in accordance with Truth before he has overcome the slavery of his body? As the intricate subtleties of language cannot be apprehended and wielded before the alphabet and the simplest words are mastered, neither can the deep subtleties of the mind be understood and purified before the A B C of right conduct is perfectly acquired. As for the labor involved—does not the youth joyfully and patiently submit himself to a seven-years' apprenticeship in order to master a craft? And does he not day by day carefully and faithfully carry out every detail of his master's instructions, looking forward to the time when, perfected through obedience and practice, he shall be himself a master? Where is the man who sincerely aims at excellence in music, painting, literature, in any trade, business, or profession who is not willing to give his whole life to the acquirement of his particular perfection? Shall labor, then, be considered where the very highest excellence is concerned—the excellence of Truth? He who says, "The Path which you point out is too difficult; I must have Truth without labor, salvation without effort," that man will not find his way out of the confusions and sufferings of selfhood; he will not find the calm and well-fortified mind and the wisely ordered life. His love is for ease and enjoyment, and not for Truth. He who, deep in his heart, adores Truth, and aspires to know it, will consider no labor too great to be undertaken, but will adopt it joyfully and pursue it patiently, and by perseverance in practice he will come to the knowledge of Truth.

The necessity for this preliminary discipline of the body and tongue will be the more clearly perceived when it is fully understood that all these wrong outward conditions are merely the expressions of wrong conditions of heart. An indolent body means an indolent mind; an ill-regulated tongue reveals an ill-regulated mind, and the process of remedying the manifested condition is really a method of rectifying the inward state. Moreover, the overcoming of these conditions is only a small part of what is really involved in the process. The ceasing from evil leads to, and is inseparably connected with, the practice of good. While a man is overcoming indolence and self-indulgence, he is really cultivating and developing the virtues of abstinence, temperance, punctuality, and self-denial, and is acquiring that strength, energy, and resolution which are indispensable to the successful accomplishment of the higher tasks. While he is overcoming the vices of speech, he is developing the virtues of truthfulness, sincerity, reverence, kindliness, and self-control, and is gaining that mental steadiness and fixedness of purpose, without which the remoter subtleties of the mind cannot be regulated, and the higher stages of conduct and enlightenment cannot be reached. Also, as he has to do right, his knowledge deepens, and his insight is intensified, and as the child's heart is glad when his school task is mastered, so with each victory achieved, the man of virtue experiences a bliss which the seeker after pleasure and excitement can never know.

And now we come to the third lesson in the Higher Life, which consists in practising and mastering, in one's daily life, three great fundamental. Virtues—(1) Unselfish Performance of Duty; (2) Unswerving Rectitude; and (3) Unlimited Forgiveness. Having prepared the mind by overcoming the more surface and chaotic conditions mentioned in the two first lessons, the striver after Virtue and Truth is now ready to enter upon greater and more difficult tasks, and to control and purify the deeper motives of the heart. Without the right performance of duty, the higher virtues cannot be known, and Truth cannot be apprehended. Duty is generally regarded as an irksome labor, a compulsory something which must be toiled through, or be in some way circumvented. This way of regarding Duty proceeds from a selfish condition of mind, and a wrong understanding of life. All duty should be regarded as sacred, and its faithful and unselfish performance one of the leading rules of conduct. All personal and selfish considerations should be extracted and cast away from the doing of one's duty, and when this is done, Duty ceases to be irksome, and becomes joyful. Duty is only irksome to him who craves some selfish enjoyment or benefit for himself. Let the man who is chafing under the irksomeness of his duty look to himself, and he will find that his wearisomeness proceeds, not from the duty itself, but from his selfish desire to escape it. He who neglects duty, be it great or small, or of a public or private nature, neglects Virtue; he who in his heart rebels against Duty, rebels against Virtue. When Duty has become a thing of love, and when every particular duty is done accurately, faithfully, and dispassionately, there is much subtle selfishness removed from the heart, and a great step is taken toward the heights of Truth. The virtuous man concentrates his mind on the perfect doing of his own duty, and does not interfere with the duty of another.

The second step in the third lesson is the practice of Unswerving Rectitude. This Virtue must be firmly established in the mind, and so enter into every detail of man's life. All dishonesty, deception, trickery, and misrepresentation must be for ever put away, and the heart be purged of every vestige of insincerity and subterfuge. The least swerving from the path of rectitude is a deviation from Virtue. There must be no extravagance and exaggeration of speech, but the simple truth should be stated. Engaging in deception, no matter how apparently insignificant, for vain-glory, or with the hope of personal advantage, is a state of delusion which one should make efforts to dispel. It is demanded of the man of Virtue that he shall not only practice the most rigid honesty in thought, word, and deed, but that he shall be exact in his statements, omitting and adding nothing to the actual truth. In thus shaping his mind to the principle of Rectitude, he will gradually come to deal with people and things in a just and impartial spirit, considering equity before himself, and viewing all things with freedom from personal bias, passion, and prejudice. When the Virtue of Rectitude is fully practiced, acquired, and comprehended, so that all temptation to untruthfulness and insincerity has ceased, then is the heart made purer and nobler, then is character strengthened, and knowledge enlarged, and life takes on a new meaning and a new power. Thus is the second step accomplished.

The third step is the practice of Unlimited Forgiveness. This consists in overcoming the sense of injury which springs from vanity, selfishness, and pride; and in exercising disinterested charity and large-heartedness toward all. Spite, retaliation, and revenge are so utterly ignoble, and so small and foolish, as to be altogether unworthy of being noticed or harbored. No one who fosters such conditions in his heart can lift himself above folly and suffering, and guide his life aright. Only by casting them away, and ceasing to be moved by them, can a man's eyes be opened to the true way in life; only by developing a forgiving and charitable spirit can he hope to approach and perceive the strength and beauty of a well-ordered life. In the heart of the strongly virtuous man no feeling of personal injury can arise; he has put away all retaliation, and has no enemies; and if men should constitute themselves his enemies, he will regard them kindly, understanding their ignorance, and making full allowance for it. When this state of heart is arrived at, then is the third step in the discipline of one's self-seeking inclinations accomplished; then is the third great lesson in Virtue and Knowledge learned and mastered.

Having thus laid down the first ten steps and three lessons in right-doing and right-knowing, I leave those of my readers who are prepared for them to learn and master them in their everyday life. There is, of course, a still higher discipline of the body, a more far-reaching discipline of the tongue, and greater and more all-embracing virtues to acquire and understand before the highest state of bliss and knowledge can be apprehended, but it is not my purpose to deal with them here. I have expounded only the first and easiest lessons on the Higher Path, and by the time these are thoroughly mastered, the reader will have become so purified, strengthened, and enlightened, that he will not be left in the dark as to his future progress. Those of my readers who have completed these three lessons will already have perceived, beyond and above, the high altitudes of Truth, and the narrow and precipitous track which leads to them, and will choose whether they shall proceed.

The straight Path which I have laid down can be pursued by all with greater profit to themselves and to the world, and even those who do not aspire to the attainment of Truth, will develop greater intellectual and moral strength, finer judgment, and deeper peace of mind by perfecting themselves in this Path. Nor will their material prosperity suffer by this change of heart; nay, it will be rendered truer, purer, and more enduring, for if there is one who is capable of succeeding and fitted to achieve, it is the man who has abandoned the petty dissipations and everyday vices of his kind, who is strong to rule his body and his mind, and who pursues with fixed resolve the path of unswerving integrity and sterling virtue.

Mental Conditions
and Their Effects

Without going into the details of the greater steps and lessons in the right life (a task outside the scope of this small work) a few hints and statements concerning those mental conditions from which life in its totality springs, will prove helpful to those who are ready and willing to penetrate further into that inner realm of heart and mind where Love and Wisdom and Peace await the strenuous comer.

All sin is ignorance. It is a condition of darkness and undevelopment. The wrong-thinker and wrong-doer is in the same position in the school of life as is the ignorant pupil in the school of learning. He has yet to learn how to think and act correctly, that is, in accordance with Law. The pupil in learning is not happy so long as he does his lessons wrongly, and unhappiness cannot be escaped while sin remains unconquered.

Life is a series of lessons. Some are diligent in learning them, and they become pure, wise, and altogether happy. Others are negligent, and do not apply themselves, and they remain impure, foolish, and unhappy.

Every form of unhappiness springs from a wrong condition of mind. Happiness inheres in right conditions of mind. Happiness is mental harmony; unhappiness is mental inharmony. While a man lives in wrong conditions of mind, he will live a wrong life, and will suffer continually. Suffering is rooted in error. Bliss inheres in enlightenment. There is salvation for man only in the destruction of his own ignorance, error, and self-delusion. Where there are wrong conditions of mind there is bondage and unrest; where there are right conditions of mind there is freedom and peace.

Here are some of the leading wrong mental conditions and their disastrous effects upon the life:

Wrong Mental Conditions	Their Effects
Hatred	Injury, violence, disaster, and suffering.
Lust	Confusion of intellect, remorse, shame, and wretchedness.
Covetousness	Fear, unrest, unhappiness, and loss.
Pride	Disappointment, chagrin, lack of self-knowledge.
Vanity	Distress, and mortification of spirit.

Condemnation	Persecution, hatred from others.
Ill-will	Failures and troubles.
Self-indulgence	Misery, loss of judgment, grossness, disease, and neglect.
Anger	Loss of power and influence.
Desire, or Self-slavery	Grief, folly, sorrow, uncertainty, and loneliness.

The above wrong conditions of mind are merely negations; they are states of darkness and deprivation and not of positive power. Evil is not a power; it is ignorance and misuse of good. The hater is he who has failed to do the lesson of Love correctly, and he suffers in consequence. When he succeeds in doing it rightly, the hatred will have disappeared, and he will see and understand the darkness and impotence of hatred. It is so with every wrong condition.

The chart on the following lists some of the more important right mental conditions and their beneficent effects upon the life.

These conditions of mind are states of positive power, of light, of joyful possession, and of knowledge. The good man knows. He has learned to do his lessons correctly, and thereby understands the exact proportions which make up the sum of life. He is enlightened, and knows good and evil. He is supremely happy, doing only that which is divinely right.

The man who is involved in the wrong conditions of mind, does not know. He is ignorant of good and evil, of himself, of the inward causes which make his life. He is unhappy, and believes other people are entirely the cause of his unhappiness. He works blindly, and lives in darkness, seeing no central purpose in existence, and no orderly and lawful sequence in the course of things.

Right Mental Conditions	Their Effects
Love	Gentle conditions, bliss, and blessedness.
Purity	Intellectual clearness, joy, invincible confidence.
Selflessness	Courage, satisfaction, happiness, and plenty.
Humility	Calmness, restfulness, knowledge of Truth.
Meekness	Equipoise, contentment under all circumstances.
Compassion	Protection, love and reverence from others.
Goodwill	Gladness and success.
Self-control	Peace of mind, true judgment, refinement, health, and honor.
Patience	Mental power, far-reaching influence.
Self-conquest	Enlightenment, wisdom, insight, and profound peace.

He who aspires to the attainment of the Higher Life in its completion—who would perceive with unveiled vision the true order of things and the meaning of life—let him abandon all the wrong conditions of heart, and persevere unceasingly in the practice of the good. If he suffers, or doubts, or is unhappy, let him search within until he finds the cause, and having found it, let him cast it away. Let him so guard and purify his heart that every day less of evil and more of good shall issue therefrom; so will he daily become stronger, nobler, wiser; so will his blessedness increase, and the Light of Truth, growing ever brighter and brighter within him, will dispel all gloom, and illuminate his Pathway.

Exhortation

Disciples of Truth, lovers of Virtue, seekers of Wisdom; ye, also, who are sorrow stricken, knowing the emptiness of the self-life, and who aspire to the life that is supremely beautiful, and serenely glad, take now yourselves in hand, enter the Door of Discipline, and know the Better Life.

Put away self-delusion; behold yourself as you are, and see the Path of Virtue as it is. There is no lazy way to Truth. He who would stand upon the mountain's summit must strenuously climb, and must rest only to gather strength. But if the climbing is less glorious than the cloudless summit, it is still glorious. Discipline in itself is beautiful, and the end of discipline is sweet.

Rise early and meditate. Begin each day with a conquered body, and a mind fortified against error and weakness. Temptation will never be overcome by unprepared fighting. The mind must be armed and arrayed in the silent hour. It must be trained to perceive, to know, to understand. Sin and temptation disappear when right understanding is developed.

Right understanding is reached through unabated discipline. Truth cannot be reached but through discipline. Patience will increase by effort and practice, and patience will make discipline beautiful.

Discipline is irksome to the impatient man and the self-lover, so he avoids it, and continues to live loosely and confusedly.

Discipline is not irksome to the Truth-lover, and he will find the Infinite patience which can wait and work and overcome. As the joy of the gardener who sees his flowers develop day by day, so is the joy of the man of discipline who sees the divine flowers of Purity, Wisdom, Compassion, and Love, grow up in his heart.

The loose-liver cannot escape sorrow and pain. The undisciplined mind falls, weak and helpless, before the fierce onslaught of passion.

Array well your mind, then, lover of Truth. Be watchful, thoughtful, resolute. Your salvation is at hand; your readiness and effort are all that are needed. If you should fail ten times, do not be disheartened; if you should fail a hundred times, rise up and pursue your way; if you should fail a thousand times, do not despair. When the right Path is entered, success is sure if the Path is not utterly abandoned.

First strife, and then victory. First labor, and then rest. First weakness, and then strength. In the beginning the lower life, and the glare and confusion of battle, and at the end the Life Beautiful, the Silence, and the Peace.

No selection of James Allen's work would be represen-tative without including a piece of the long-form poetry to which he also dedicated himself. Allen, like his older contemporary Edwin Arnold (1832-1904), brought Buddhist ideas to a general readership who, prior to Arnold's Light of Asia *and early Theosophical works, had heard little of the ancient traditions of the East.*

—MH

Buddha

Under Mount Ratnagira's western shade,
Weary and worn with his long search for Truth,
Sorrowing, unsatisfied, disconsolate,
Sat Buddha, knowing not where he should turn
To find the Truth that he had so long sought—
The Truth that maketh steadfast, strong, and pure,
The Truth that bringeth peace and blessed rest.
The Schools had failed him; the philosophies,
Hoary and ancient, had not stilled the cry
Of passion in his heart; and passion's child,
Sorrow, was with him still; the scriptures, creeds,
Proud pillars of the State, had failed to bear
The weight of his great woe, crumbling away
Under temptation, leaving him the prey
Still of desire and pain and clouded mind.
Mortifications he had tried, and they
Had left him strengthless, wan, wanting the Truth;
And now he seemed as one defeated, borne
Upon the stream of Fate, helpless, alone.

But while the Buddha brooded in the shade,
Suddenly on his ear there fell a cry,
A sob of pain, a pitiful strange sigh;
Whereat he rose, and left the shade, and sought
(He scarce knew why, but that there leaped within
His sorrowing heart a mighty unknown love)
Whence came the cry; and presently he saw,
Upon the road, 'mid thirsty clouds of dust,
Under the fierce blaze of the Indian sun,
A shepherd, driving hard a flock of sheep;
And in the rear there lagged a little lamb
With wounded feet, bleating most piteously,
The while the ewe, with anguish deep and sore,
Cried o'er her little one, knowing that she
Was helpless to relieve her.

                              When Buddha saw
The piteous spectacle, compassion slew
His own deep sorrow; and he straightway took
The wounded lamb, and bore it in his arms,
Saying, "Vain are the strivings of the soul
After vain knowledge; vain the learned lore
That hath not pity in it; vain is life
That hath not love; and whatsoe'er is false,

And what uncertain, though it seemeth true,
This thing is true, that I should pity thee.
The priests who pray and read, and read and pray,

Die in their sins at last, and do not find
The Love I mourn for, the deep Truth I seek;
And better were it that I ease thy pain
Than pray with them, and seek and never find.
Thee will I love; yes, I will pity thee
Whom none will pity; thee will I relieve;
Tired of the soulless theories of men,
I, Buddha, will stoop to thee, thou dumb, weak thing,
Whom men despise, knowing that this is true,
Whate'er is doubtful, and whate'er unsure,
Pity and Love are right; whatever fades
And perishes, Compassion will not fade,
And Love will never perish." So he took
Into his arms the weary, wounded thing
Which nestled in his bosom, and became
Quiet and peaceful; and the anxious ewe
Walked by his side, looking into his face,
Glad that her lamb had found those blessed arms:
And so she walked, and dumbly worshipped him,
Knowing him Buddha, the compassionate.

And Buddha in that hour entered the Way
Which he had vainly sought in schools and creeds;
Entered the Path which no philosophy
Leads unto, and which none shall ever find
But by sweet deeds of Love, forgetting self;
And in his heart there grew a holy Love;
And in his mind a knowledge new and strange;

And his whole being felt a painless peace;
Sorrow and pain were not; and then he knew
That he had found the holy Truth at last.

And from thenceforward Buddha lived the Truth,
And taught its practice; and from far and near
Came men and women who had sought the Truth,
And at his feet they sat and worshipped him,
Learning of love and pity; finding bliss
And peace that cannot fail; and him they called
Deliverer, Redeemer, Blessed Lord.
And even they who understood not, sensed
Faintly this truth which one day they should know:
Better than learning is a loving heart;
And to give comfort to one wounded lamb
Is higher than the wisdom of the schools,
And greater than the world's philosophy.

IX
"Thoroughness"

(from *Mastery of Destiny*, 1909)

This piece serves as an excellent adjunct to the earlier essay "Small Tasks and Duties." Allen provides what I consider a vital and underestimated observation: "He who lacks thoroughness in his worldly duties, will also lack the same quality in spiritual things." That is the kind of statement with which one immediately wants to argue. Aren't we taught to "seek first the kingdom of God?" Well, look again. Allen makes the important point that until an individual can be trusted with "small tasks" he cannot be trusted with ultimate questions of life. The behavior that a person displays toward earthly obligations—which involve service, trust, and fealty to others—will repeat itself in matters of the spiritual search. Although Allen doesn't quote the principle in this chapter, he sheds light on Christ's observation, "the children of darkness are wiser in their day than the children of light." (Luke 16:8)   —MH

Thoroughness

Thoroughness consists in doing little things as though they were the greatest things in the world. That the little things of life are of primary importance, is a truth not generally understood, and the thought that little things can be neglected, thrown aside, or slurred over, is at the root of that lack of thoroughness which is so common, and which results in imperfect work and unhappy lives.

When one understands that the great things of the world and of life consist of a combination of small things, and that without this aggregation of small things the great things would be nonexistent, then he begins to pay careful attention to those things which he formerly regarded as insignificant. He thus acquires the quality of thoroughness, and becomes a man of usefulness and influence; for the possession or non-possession of this one quality may mean all the difference between a life of peace and power, and one of misery and weakness.

Every employer of labor knows how comparatively rare this quality is—how difficult it is to find men and women who will put thought and energy into their work, and do it completely and satisfactorily. Bad workmanship abounds. Skill and excellence are acquired by few. Thoughtlessness, carelessness, and laziness are such common vices that it should cease to appear strange that, in spite of "social reform," the ranks of the unemployed should continue to swell, for those who scamp their work today will, another day, in the hour of deep necessity, look and ask for work in vain.

The law of "the survival of the fittest" is not based on cruelty, it is based on justice; it is one aspect of that divine equity which everywhere prevails. Vice is "beaten with many stripes"; if it were not so, how could virtue be developed? The thoughtless and lazy cannot take precedence of, or stand equally with, the thoughtful and industrious. A friend of mine tells me that his father gave all his children the following piece of advice:

> *Whatever your future work may be, put your whole mind upon it and do it thoroughly; you need then have no fear as to your welfare, for there are so many who are careless and negligent that the services of the thorough man are always in demand.*

I know those who have, for years, tried almost in vain to secure competent workmanship in spheres which do not require exceptional skill, but which call chiefly for forethought, energy, and conscientious care. They have discharged one after another for negligence, laziness, incompetence, and persistent breaches of duty—not to mention other vices which have no bearing on this subject; yet the vast army of the unemployed continues to cry out against the laws, against society, and against Heaven.

The cause of this common lack of thoroughness is not far to seek; it lies in that thirst for pleasure which not only creates a distaste for steady labor, but renders one incapable of doing the best work, and of properly fulfilling one's duty. A short time ago, a case came under my observation (one of many such), of a poor woman who was given, at her earnest appeal, a responsible and lucrative position. She had been at her post only a few days when she began to talk of the "pleasure trips" she was going to have now she had come to that place. She was discharged at the end of a month for negligence and incompetence.

As two objects cannot occupy the same space at the same time, so the mind that is occupied with pleasure cannot also be concentrated upon the perfect performance of duty. Pleasure has its own place and time, but its consideration should not be allowed to enter the mind during those hours which should be devoted to duty. Those who, while engaged in their worldly task, are continually dwelling upon anticipated pleasures, cannot do otherwise than bungle through their work, or even neglect it when their pleasure seems to be at stake.

Thoroughness is completeness, perfection; it means doing a thing so well that there is nothing left to be desired; it means doing one's work, if not better than anyone else can do it, at least not worse than the best that others do. It means the exercise of much thought, the putting forth of great energy, the persistent application of the mind to its task, the cultivation of patience, perseverance, and a high sense of duty. An ancient teacher said, "If anything has to be done, let a man do it, let him attack it vigorously"; and another teacher said, "Whatsoever thy hand findeth to do, do it with thy might."

He who lacks thoroughness in his worldly duties, will also lack the same quality in spiritual things. He will not improve his character; will be weak and half-hearted in his religion, and will not accomplish any good and useful end. The man who keeps one eye on worldly pleasure and the other on religion, and who thinks he can have the advantage of both conditions, will not be thorough either in his pleasure-seeking or his religion, but will make a sorry business of both. It is better to be a whole-souled worldling than a half-hearted religionist; better to give the entire mind to a lower thing than half of it to a higher.

It is preferable to be thorough, even if it be in a bad or selfish direction, rather than inefficient and squeamish in good directions, for thoroughness leads more rapidly to the development of character and the acquisition of wisdom; it accelerates progress and unfoldment; and while it leads the bad to something better, it spurs the good to higher and ever higher heights of usefulness and power.

X

"Light on the Management of the Mind"

——✦❧❈☙✦——

(from *Light on Life's Difficulties*, 1912)

In this brief chapter Allen explores how we can allow the frictions that we experience with others to serve as a goad to self-improvement rather than an excuse for our own failures. This is one of Allen's final writings before his death in early 1912.   —MH

Light on the Management
of the Mind

F ollowing the last chapter a few hints on the manage-
ment of one's mind will doubtless be opportune. Before
a man can see even the necessity for thorough and complete
self-government, he will have to throw off a great delusion
in which so many are involved—the delusion of believing
that his lapses of conduct are due to those about him, and
not entirely to himself. "I could make far greater progress
if I were not hindered by others," or "It is impossible for me
to make any headway, seeing that I live with such irritable
people," are commonly expressed complaints which spring
from the error of imagining that others are responsible for
one's own folly.

The violent or irritable man always blames those about
him for his fits of anger, and by continually living in this
delusion, he becomes more and more confirmed in his rash-
ness and perturbations, for how can a man overcome—nay,

how can he even try to overcome, his weakness if he convinces himself that it springs entirely from the actions of others? Moreover, firmly believing this, as he does, he vents his anger more and more upon others in order to try and make matters better for himself, and so becomes completely lost to all knowledge of the real origin of his unhappy state.

> *Men cast the blame of their unprosperous acts*
> *Upon the abettors of their own resolve,*
> *Or anything but their weak guilty selves.*

All a man's weaknesses and sins and falls take their rise in his own heart, and he alone is responsible for them. It is true there are tempters and provokers, but temptations and provocations are powerless to him who refuses to respond to them. Tempters and provokers are but foolish men, and he who gives way to them has become a willing co-operator in their folly; he is unwise and weak, and the source of his troubles is in himself. The pure man cannot be tempted; the wise man cannot be provoked.

Let a man fully realize that he is absolutely responsible for his every action, and he has already gone a considerable distance along the path which leads to wisdom and peace, for he will then commence to utilize temptation as a means of growth, and the wrong conduct of others he will regard as a test of his own strength.

Socrates thanked the gods for the gift of a shrewish wife in that it enabled him the better to cultivate the virtue of patience; and it is a simple and easily perceived truth that we can the better grow patient by living with the impatient, better grow unselfish by living with the selfish. If a man is impatient with the impatient, he is himself impatient; if he is selfish with the selfish, then he is himself selfish. The test and measure of virtue is trial, and, like gold and precious stones, the more it is tested the brighter it shines. If a man thinks he has a virtue, yet gives way when its opposing vice is presented to him, let him not delude himself, he has not yet attained to the possession of that virtue.

If a man would rise and become a man indeed, let him cease to think the weak and foolish thought, "I am hindered by others," and let him set about to discover that he is hindered only by himself; let him realize that the giving way to another is but a revelation of his own imperfection, and lo! upon him will descend the light of wisdom, and the door of peace will open unto him, and he will soon become the conqueror of self.

The fact that a man is continually troubled and disturbed by close contact with others, is an indication that he requires such contact to impel him onward to a clearer comprehension of himself, and toward a higher and more steadfast state of mind. The very things which he regards as insurmountable hindrances will become to him the most valuable aids when he fully realizes his moral responsibility and his innate power to do right. He will then cease to blame others for his unmanly conduct, and will commence to live steadfastly under all circumstances; the scales of self-delusion will quickly fall from his eyes, and he will then see that ofttimes when he imagined himself provoked by others, he himself was really the provoker; and as he rises above his own mental perturbations, the necessity for coming in contact with the same conditions in others will cease, and he will pass, by a natural process, into the company of the good and pure, and will then awaken in others the nobility which he has arrived at in himself.

> *Be noble! and the nobleness that lies*
> *In other men, sleeping, but never dead,*
> *Will rise in majesty to meet thine own.*

XI
"Good Results"

———❖———

(from *Foundation Stones to Happiness and Success*,
posthumously published 1913)

In this posthumously published work, Allen reminds the reader of the psychological symmetry behind life's outer events. The first cause is always mind, thought, and character. This outlook can provide the reader with a tremendous sense of freedom, which Allen alludes to in the foreword of As A Man Thinketh: *"They themselves are makers of themselves."*   —MH

Good Results

A considerable portion of the happenings of life come to us without any *direct* choosing on our part, and such happenings are generally regarded as having no relation to our will or character, but as appearing fortuitously, as occurring without a cause. Thus one is spoken of as being "lucky," and another "unlucky," the inference being that each has received something which he never earned, never caused. Deeper thought and a clearer insight into life convince us, however, that nothing happens without a cause, and that cause and effect are always related in perfect adjustment and harmony. This being so, every happening directly affecting us is intimately related to our own will and character, is, indeed, an effect justly related to a cause having its seat in our consciousness. In a word, involuntary happenings of life are the results of our own thoughts and deeds. This, I admit, is not apparent on the surface, but what fundamental law, even in the physical universe, is so apparent? If thought, investigation, and experiment are necessary to the discovery of the principles which relate one material atom to another, even so are they imperative to the perception and understanding of the mode of action which relate one mental condition to another; and such modes, such laws, are known by the right-doer, by him who has acquired an understanding mind by the practice of true actions.

We reap as we sow. Those things which come to us, though not by our own *choosing*, are by our *causing*. The drunkard did not choose the delirium tremens or insanity which overtook him, but he caused it by his own deeds. In this case the law is plain to all minds, but where it is not so plain, it is none the less true. Within ourselves is the deep-seated cause of all our sufferings, the spring of all our joys. Alter the inner world of thoughts, and the outer world of events will cease to bring you sorrow; make the heart pure, and to you all things will be pure, all occurrences happy and in true order.

> *Within yourselves deliverance must be sought,*
> *Each man his prison makes.*
> *Each hath such lordship as the loftiest ones;*
> *Nay, for with Powers above, around, below*
> *As with all flesh and whatsoever lives,*
> *Act maketh joy or woe.*

Our life is good or bad, enslaved or free, according to its causation in our thoughts, for out of these thoughts spring all our deeds; and from these deeds come equitable results.

We cannot seize good results violently, like a thief, and claim and enjoy them, but we can bring them to pass by setting in motion the causes within ourselves.

Men strive for money, sigh for happiness, and would gladly possess wisdom, yet fail to secure these things, while they see others to whom these blessings appear to come unbidden. The reason is that they have generated causes which prevent the fulfillment of their wishes and efforts.

Each life is a perfectly woven net-work of causes and effects, of efforts (or lack of efforts) and results, and good results can only be reached by initiating good efforts, good causes. The doer of true actions, who pursues sound methods grounded on right principles, will not need to strive and struggle for good results; they will be there as the effects of his righteous rule of life. He will reap the fruit of his own actions and the reaping will be in gladness and peace.

This truth of sowing and reaping in the moral sphere is a simple one, yet men are slow to understand and accept it. We have been told by a Wise One that "the children of darkness are wiser in their day than the children of light," and who would expect, in the material world, to reap and eat where he had not sown and planted? Or who would expect to reap wheat in the field where he had sown tares, and would fall to weeping and complaining if he did not? Yet this is just what men do in the spiritual field of mind and deed. They do evil, and expect to get from it good, and when the bitter harvesting comes in all its ripened fullness, they fall into despair, and bemoan the hardness and injustice of their lot, usually attributing it to the evil deeds of others, refusing even to admit the possibility of its cause being hidden in themselves, in their own thoughts and deeds. The children of light—those who are searching for the fundamental principles of right living with a view to making themselves into wise and happy beings—must train themselves to observe this law of cause and effect in thought, word and deed, as implicitly and obediently as the gardener obeys the law of sowing and reaping. He does not even question the law; he recognizes and obeys it. When the wisdom which he instinctively practices in his garden, is practiced by men in the garden of their minds— when the law of the sowing of deeds is so fully recognized that it can no longer be doubted or questioned—then it will be just as faithfully followed by the sowing of those actions which will bring about a reaping of happiness and well-being for all. As the children of matter obey the laws of matter, so let the children of spirit obey the laws of spirit, for the law of matter and the law of spirit are one; they are but two aspects of one thing; the outworking of one principle in opposite directions.

If we observe right principles or causes, wrong effects cannot possibly accrue. If we pursue sound methods, no shoddy thread can find its way into the web of our life, no rotten brick enter into the building of our character to render it insecure; and if we do true actions, what but good results can come to pass; for to say that good causes can produce bad effects is to say that nettles can be reaped from a sowing of corn.

He who orders his life along the moral lines thus briefly enunciated, will attain to such a state of insight and equilibrium as to render him permanently happy and perennially glad; all his efforts will be seasonably planted; all the issues of his life will be good, and though he may not become a millionaire—as indeed he will have no desire to become such—he will acquire the gift of peace, and true success will wait upon him as its commanding master.

James Allen Timeline

1864
James Allen is born on November 28, 1864 at 21 Brunswick Street, in Leicester, England, to parents William and Martha. His family later adds two younger brothers, George and Thomas.

1879
William Allen departs to find work in America. Shortly before Christmas, news reaches home that William has been killed a murder-robbery in New York City. James, newly fifteen, must leave school to support the family through factory knit work.

1889
James finds new employment as a secretary and stationer in London.

1895
James weds Lily Louisa Oram, born 1867.

1896

Lily gives birth to their only daughter, Nora.

1898

James begins writing for the journal *The Herald of the Golden Age*.

1901

James publishes his first book, *From Poverty to Power*.

1902

James founds his own magazine, *The Light of Reason*, later called *The Epoch*.

1903

James publishes *All These Things Added* and his landmark work *As a Man Thinketh*. Soon after Allen family moves to the southern English coastal town of Ilfracombe.

1904

Publishes *Byways of Blessedness* and *Out from the Heart*.

1907

Publishes *Poems of Peace* and *The Life Triumphant*.

1908

Publishes *Morning and Evening Thoughts* and *Through the Gate of Good*.

1909

Publishes *The Mastery of Destiny*.

1910

Publishes *Above Life's Turmoil* and *From Passion to Peace*.

1911

Publishes *Man: King of Mind, Body, and Circumstance* and *Eight Pillars of Prosperity*. James's health begins to falter late in the year.

1912

James dies at home in Ilfracombe on January 24, probably from tuberculosis. He is cremated on January 30, with his brother Thomas scattering the ashes. James's *Light on Life's Difficulties* appears posthumously that year. Lily writes a memorial to her husband in the February-March issue of *The Epoch*.

1913

Lily continues publishing *The Epoch* and founds the New Thought-oriented society, the Union of Right Thinking. Lily issues two of James's books posthumously: *Foundation Stones to Happiness and Success* and *James Allen's Book of Meditations for Every Day in the Year*.

1914

Lily posthumously issues James's *Men and Systems*, a book that advocates humane working conditions.

1915

Lily publishes the last of James's posthumous works, *The Shining Gateway*. In years ahead she continues producing

The Epoch and her own writing. She maintains salons and opens the Allen home as a guesthouse.

1952
Lily dies on February 14.

1976
Nora, a Spiritualist and later a devout Roman Catholic, dies July 18, 1976. Never married, Nora had maintained the family home in Ilfracombe and rented rooms to single women.

About the Authors

JAMES ALLEN was born in Leicester, England, on November 28, 1864. He took his first job at fifteen to support his family, after his father was murdered while looking for work in America in 1879. Allen worked as a factory knitter and later as a private secretary with various manufacturing companies. In 1901, he published his first book, *From Poverty to Power*. The following year, he left secretarial work to devote himself full time to writing and in 1903 completed his third, and best-known, work: *As a Man Thinketh*. Allen soon moved with his wife, Lily, and daughter, Nora, to Ilfracombe, England, where he continued to write books and articles, and, with Lily, to publish his spiritual journal, *The Light of Reason*, later retitled *The Epoch*. He died at age forty-seven on January 24, 1912, most likely of tuberculosis. Allen completed nineteen books during his career, several of which were published posthumously by his wife. All are included in this volume. While not widely known during his lifetime, Allen came to be seen as pioneering voice of contemporary inspirational literature, his work inspiring many of the twentieth century's leading writers of motivational thought, including Norman Vincent Peale, Napoleon Hill, Robert Collier, and Dale Carnegie.

MITCH HOROWITZ is one of today's most literate voices of self-help and alternative spirituality. *The Washington Post* writes that Mitch "treats esoteric ideas and movements with an even-handed intellectual studiousness that is too often lost in today's raised-voice discussions." Mitch is the PEN Award-winning author of books including *Occult America*, *One Simple Idea*, *The Miracle Club*, *Secrets of Self-Mastery*, and *The Miracle Habits*. He received the Walden Award for Interfaith/Intercultural Understanding. The Chinese government has censored his work. Visit him on Twitter @MitchHorowitz and on Instagram @MitchHorowitz23.

9 781722 501488